AMERICAN PLAINS BISON

* * *

REWILDING AN ICON

James A. Bailey

sweetgrassbooks
a division of Farcountry Press

2013

You may order extra copies of this book by calling Farcountry Press toll free at (800) 821-3874. Produced by Sweetgrass Books; PO Box 5630, Helena, MT 59604; (800) 821-3874; www.sweetgrassbooks.com

Cover Design and book layout by Kathryn QannaYahu

Printed in the United States

ISBN 10: 1-59152-123-8

ISBN 13: 978-1-59152-123-5

with support from:

Center for Biological Diversity

Wildearth Guardians

Gallatin Wildlife Association

William Mealer, MD

Yellowstone Buffalo Foundation

Upper Missouri River Guides

Natural Resources Defense Council

Table of Contents

Charts, Maps and Figures

Charts

Maps

7.3 Portion of Badlands National Park including an area with 600 bison.

7.4 Federal public multiple-use land (Kiowa National Grassland) north of Roy, in northeast New Mexico.

7.5 In Nevada, Ruby Lakes National Wildlife Refuge is surrounded by a vast area of other federal, multiple-use land managed by the Bureau of Land Management and Forest Service.

7.6 Mostly federal multiple-use land and some state land surrounding Malheur Lakes and Hart Mountain National Wildlife Refuges.

Figures

1.1 Steppe bison, *Bison priscus*, was the first bison in North America.

1.2 Steppe bison display at University of Alaska Museum.

1.3 Steppe bison skull from 36,000-year old specimen.

1.4 A comparison of modern bison and giant bison (*Bison latifrons*) bulls.

2.1 An estimated 250,000 bison hides piled for shipment from Dodge City, Kansas in 1874.

2.2 Buffalo, Oklahoma, on Buffalo Creek, has not seen a wild bison in many decades.

3.1 Summary of processes leading toward three forms of extinction of wild plains bison on native range in the USA.

4.1 The lower critical temperature of a bison is about minus 40 degrees.

4.2 Newborn bison calves are precocial, standing within minutes and able to run within hours.

4.3 Bison bull testing cow for reproductive status.

4.4 Bison bulls tending cows during the Yellowstone rutting season.

4.5 Wallowing, an important social behavior of bison, influences the microhydrology and plant composition of bison habitat.

4.6 Bison bulls in a brief dominance dispute.

5.1 Older bison bulls typically travel alone or with only a few other bulls during most of the year.

5.2 Except during the rut, most bison travel in large mixed groups of cows, calves, yearlings, and a few young bulls.

5.3 Bison group sizes are normally largest during the rut.

5.4 Note the pair of bison competing for one small patch of forage.

6.1 Tourists line up to observe the bison herd.

6.2 Bison attract tourists and support local economies.

6.3 Bison in art, depicting pair on the windy Great Plains.

6.4 A few among several thousand who spent their recreation dollars observing the Custer State Park bison roundup in 2010.

6.5 The "bison circus" at Custer State Park, South Dakota.

7.1 Across the western Great Plains, relics persist from an agrarian human population that has been declining for almost 100 years.

7.2 With declining human populations, many small towns of the Great Plains have fallen on hard economic times.

7.3 Much of the land in Badlands National Park is poor or mediocre bison habitat, devoid of vegetation.

8.1 Six of the 10 large grazing mammals that are abundant in domestication but uncommon or rare in the wild.

8.2 Bison being processed during the annual roundup, Custer State Park, South Dakota.

8.3 The Custer State Park conservation herd of bison is rounded up and processed for handling and culling annually.

8.4 Ear tags diminish esthetic value of wild bison. Broken and deformed horns are a common result of frequent handling.

8.5 "Wild" bison being fed in holding pens within Yellowstone National Park during 2011.

9.1 In 1907, Bronx Zoo staff sent 15 bison by rail to Wichita Mountains Wildlife Preserve, Oklahoma.

Introduction

There are two kinds of American bison. Wood bison were originally in the north and plains bison, subject of this book, occupied much of southern Canada, the contiguous United States and a little of Mexico. Plains bison is something of a misnomer, as the former range of these animals included far more than the Great Plains. However, written history emphasizes the saga of bison on the Plains to an extent that few Americans think of bison anywhere else. The danger is that a narrow view of bison history, and the name "plains" bison, may constrain our vision of where bison could or should be restored as wild animals. (Much the same is true for "Rocky Mountain" elk and for wild "mountain" sheep.)

A lot has been written about the past of wild bison in North America, and a fair amount has been written about the present status of bison. However, too little has been written about the future of wild bison. In my reading, three authors have shown the way:

No matter how good the intentions are, holding more bison behind more fences is a stopgap measure at best and not a lasting answer to conservation. Large herds on large tracts of land and little hindered by fences are more likely to remain close to the native genotype of bison. [1]   Valerius Geist

Bison domestication will strip out the genes that make for good domestic bison and discard the genes that make wild bison wild. To keep bison wild you must be willing to lose money on them – or at least leave money on the table. Only the public can afford to do that, and only as publicly owned animals do wild bison have a future. [2]
                    Dale Lott

In addition, in writing mostly about the bison of Yellowstone National Park, Mary Ann Franke wrote:

The bison that now roams Yellowstone has a life on the edge – the edge between the wild animal it still is and the zoolike exhibit it could become if subjected to the kind of livestock management practices

Introduction

typically applied to bison herds.[3]

And Dale Lott wrote: Plains bison are *"the only wild animal in the United States that is not allowed to live as a wild animal – live outside parks and refuges – anywhere in its original range."*[2]

More than a decade ago, Ernest Callenbach[4] wrote of bison restoration on the Great Plains. However, loss of genetic integrity and domestication of bison had not yet been widely discussed as threats to the future of wild bison.

More recently, bison biologists wrote: "In the absence of intentional policies and actions to conserve the wild character and genome of bison, captivity and commercialization can lead inadvertently or intentionally to a variety of effects that may be deleterious to bison as a wildlife species in the intermediate or long term."[5]

Today, we have scientists debating how large a bison population is needed to retain all or most of its diversity of genetic material. Genetic diversity is necessary for a species to continue to evolve and adapt to future environments. There is debate over how much genetic diversity will be needed; and over how to reduce the need for large gene pools by moving animals among herds. In contrast, there is too little thought given to what the future environments of bison will be. These environments will include both natural and human-caused selection that will determine the future of the bison genome.

We do not leave bison to future generations of Americans. We leave the bison genome. Bison die, but their genes persist across generations. Thus the complex and somewhat technical concepts of conservation genetics must be addressed. What selective forces will shape the bison we leave to succeeding generations? For what purpose are we saving genetic diversity of bison?

Aside from commercial bison producers, bison are most valuable to the public as wild animals. Wild bison have historical, recreational, aesthetic, economic, ecologic, social and cultural values that depend upon their most unique characteristic – wildness. So I write about the future of wildness in bison.

Introduction

My intention is to describe some details of the breadth and depth of wildness in American plains bison, and to show how bison wildness is threatened by creeping domestication. Even in the so-called "conservation herds", bison are being sidetracked away from numerical extinction, but into domestication. However, domestication is extinction of the wild form. It is my hope that this book will accelerate public debate on the future of American plains bison toward having a few wild landscapes with wild bison. A nation as rich as ours can do this. We need only to generate sufficient knowledge of the issues, and sufficient perception of our obligation to future generations to save some examples of wild bison.

Humans have already domesticated many species of wild hoofed animals. These are models of what can happen to plains bison. Species of horses, pigs, sheep, goats, camels, and reindeer have been domesticated. For several of these, the progenitor species are now uncommon, rare or extinct in the wild.

True, it has taken centuries to replace most or all the wild yak, water buffalo, gaur, aurachs and banteng - progenitors of domestic forms of cattle. But these domestications must have started slowly, as we are starting now with bison. Most of our plains bison live in captivity, and all have lived under some form of human management for over a century.

Domestication is the predominant threat to persistence of wild plains bison. If wild plains bison are to persist, we must retain the wild genome in a wild environment. In an "artificial" environment with abundant human controls, the wild genome will deteriorate into something else.

I do not write for scientists, many of whom know more of bison ecology and genetics than I. Wild bison have no adequate constituency because most people think that having many herds behind fences is sufficient for all time. So I write for concerned and interested laypersons, hoping to develop a constituency for wild bison.

In some chapters, I deviate from biogeography and emphasize state boundaries – and state laws and policies affecting bison. As long as state laws and policies are the major factors limiting restoration of wild plains bison in the USA, active coalitions of state citizens will be necessary to initiate bison restoration. In that sense, this quasi-scientific document might be used as a handbook for in-state bison advocates. For more on the science of bison, they should consult the IUCN 2010 status survey of American Bison.[5]

Much of what I write has been said elsewhere in scattered books, reports and articles. I believe there is a need to put this information together in one place; to demonstrate the magnitude and complexity of the problem of creeping domestication of plains bison in the USA and to provide a focus for real restoration of wild bison.

My writing on the prehistory and history of plains bison is much abbreviated. Those interested in these subjects should see the original works. I am not a historian. But I have included enough of the grand, yet sometimes inglorious, history of bison to provide needed background for, and appreciation of, the plight of wild plains bison today.

This is not an "Oh wow!" book about bison. Such books describe the unique, intriguing and wondrous attributes of wild bison. They are important for public appreciation of why we should save wild bison. Many authors have done a superlative job in this regard. This is a book about why and how to retain wildness in bison for future generations. It is a large and complex subject, involving many states, several federal agencies and private organizations, history and prehistory, conservation philosophy and biopolitics, and the always incomplete and expanding subjects of bison biology, ecology and genetics. You may have to be very interested to plow through all of it. I have done my best to present the sometimes abstruse concepts and intermingled issues in a readable format. Redundancy is sometimes necessary with so many interrelated topics. But, I hope it is still "a good read"; and you will be the judge of that.

I have used modern place names to designate historic locations of bison. While these places, including states, often did not exist at the

Introduction

time of some bison observations, communication is best served by this simple approach. In deference to our friends in other nations of North and South America, I usually refer to the United States simply as the "USA", not as "America". Yet, I must apologize for continuing to refer to our people as "Americans". "United Statesians" is just too clumsy! Sometimes I refer to these people simply as "us", for we Americans all share this obligation to restore some wild bison for the sake of future generations of us.

Footnotes:

[1] Geist (1996)

[2] Lott (2002)

[3] Franke (2005)

[4] Callenbach (1996)

[5] Gates et al. (2010)

Acknowledgments

I am indebted to Valerius Geist and Jim Shaw for their support and encouragement. Also, Dr. Geist provided the unique sketch of an ice-age giant bison in scale with a modern bison. Additional encouragement came from friends in the Gallatin Wildlife Association and the Buffalo Field Campaign. Friend and former co-worker Don MacCarter provided the best bison photos. (The amateurish photos are mine.) My wife and long-time fellow traveler, Nan, enjoyed the trips through bison country with me during 2010-2011. As always, she provided my most valuable support.

I am grateful for the time and effort provided by bison biologists and bison managers as I gathered data on our conservation herds. These people provided friendly communications and exhibited their personal concerns for the future of wild bison:

Introduction

In the northern Great Plains: Ron Jablonski, John Kinney and Gene Degeyner, U. S. Forest Service/National Grasslands; Bryce Christensen, Jeff Hegener, American Prairie Reserve; Eric Rosenquist, Cross Ranch; Mary Miller, Ordway Prairie; Ed Childers, Badlands National Park; Dan Roddy, Wind Cave National Park; Chad Kramer, Custer State Park; Mike Oehler, Theodore Roosevelt National Park; and Wes Olsen, Grasslands National Park, Saskatchewan.

In the central Great Plains: Mike Morava, Fort Robinson State Park; Richard Egelhoff, Niobrara Valley Reserve; Steve Hicks and Kathy McPeak, Fort Niobrara National Wildlife Refuge.

In the southern Great Plains: C. L. Hawkins and Todd Montandon, Caprock State Park; Cliff Peterson, Maxwell State Wildlife Refuge; Robert Hamilton, Tallgrass Prairie Preserve; Kristin Hayes, Tallgrass Prairie National Preserve; Tom Norman, Sandsage State Bison Range; Eva Horne, Konza Prairie; Walter Munsterman, Wichita Mountains National Wildlife Refuge; Rick Hansen, Rita Blanca/Kiowa National Grasslands; Tom Ronning, Rocky Mountain Arsenal; and an anonymous respondent from Prairie State Park, Missouri.

In the Rocky Mountains and far West: Justin Shannon, Henry Mountains; Eric Cole, National Elk Refuge; Steve Cain, Grand Teton National Park; Rick Wallen, Yellowstone National Park; Dan Sharps, National Bison Range; Paul Robertson, Medano/Zapata Ranch; Martin Homola, Denver Parks; and Steve Bates, Antelope Island State Park.

Part I

Origins

The prehistoric bison lineage is long, diverse and magnificent. It is a gift from thousands of years of evolution, with bison living and dying.

Few Americans know that plains bison recently occurred in at least 40 of the 48 contiguous states.

Chapter 1

From Steppe Bison to Plains Bison

Bison are unique among North American large mammals. They are the largest, and, today, they are the most neglected by wildlife conservation. How did this happen and why should it be reversed? The answers begin in the long history of bison evolution.

Pleistocene Origins

As we plan a future for plains bison, there is much concern that we retain all or most of the species' remaining genetic diversity. This is recognition of the obvious: evolution has not ended! The bison genome will continue to adapt to future conditions. However, humans largely determine what those conditions will be, so we are determining the future of bison evolution, and what kind of bison we leave to succeeding generations. To understand this future of evolving plains bison, we must look to the past and consider what environmental conditions gave us wild bison. Moreover, even a brief understanding of bison evolution enhances one's appreciation of the grandeur of the wild beasts now in our care.

North American bison are products of the Pleistocene, a period we refer to as the "ice age". Beginning 2 million or more years ago, there have been several major glacial advances, with intervening periods of glacial retreat. The last two glacial advances are referred to as Illinoian and Wisconsin glaciers. Illinoisan glaciers reined about 130-200,000 years ago. The Sangamon interglacial intervened during 110-130,000 years ago. Wisconsin glaciers began about 110,000 years ago, lasting until 10-20,000 years before present. (All these dates, except the last, continue to be debated.)

Connections of Asia with North America, and two-way exchange of animal species, occurred in "Beringia" during glaciations with corresponding lowered sea levels. An early form of *Bison* probably entered North America during Illinoisan glaciation (Chart 1.1). Also, faunas in unglaciated portions of the north, Beringia and the Alaska-Yukon refugium, were separated from faunas of the south during glacial periods. Evolution proceeded independently during these separations. Recontact and gene flow between these faunas

Rewilding Plains Bison

Chart 1.1. Simplified view of spatial and evolutionary relations of bison in North America during the late Pleistocene to Recent period. (ybp = years before present.)

Era	Beringia, Alaska, Yukon	South Latitudes, South of Ice
Illinoian Glaciation 130-200 K ybp	**Steppe bison, *B. priscus*** from Asia, (possibly earlier) **Several large predators**	**Steppe bison** Presence questionable
Sangamon Interglacial 110-130 K ybp	**Steppe bison** isolated from Asia **Habitat reduced** (Forest encroachment)	**Steppe bison arrive** **Many large predators** **Giant bison** (*latifrons*) **Modern bison** (*antiquus*) begins
Wisconsin Glaciation 12-110 K ybp	**Steppe bison** recontact with Asia, isolated from temperate zone **Human predators** arrive late	**Bison** isolated from Steppe bison **Giant bison** extinct by 22 K ybp **Large predators** decline late **Human predators** arrive late **Warming climate late** **Smaller bison,** especially south
Recent ≤12 K ybp	**Steppe bison extinct by 10 K ybp**	**Many predators** extinct ***B. bison*** still smaller, expand north **Warming, drying** **Wood bison north** **Plains bison south**

2

occurred during inter-glacial, warmer periods, including during the Sangamon interglacial and after the last, Wisconsin, glacial retreat.

As the types of bison varied and changed across this continuum of time and space, it remains unclear whether one form of bison gradually evolved into another, or if separated forms of bison evolved independently and, upon recontact, one type replaced the other through competition, or by interbreeding and genetic swamping. The distinction is not important for my purposes. I wish to dwell upon the major natural selective forces that were operating to determine the more successful forms of bison.

Prehistoric Natural Selection. Primary selective forces during bison evolution have been competition, predation, disease, and climate with its associated effects on available forage. In response, bison evolved with changing social behaviors, predator-evasion strategies, foraging strategies, energy and nutritional efficiencies, and disease resistance. While we must think of natural selective forces separately, it is important to recognize that these forces did not act in isolation. Successful bison, those that survived and passed on their genes, had to be fit for dealing with selective forces acting simultaneously. For example, selection for body size was influenced by social competition, predator defense, a cold climate, and nutritional requirements. Adaptations of bison anatomy, physiology and behavior had to be coordinated to deal with multiple environmental opportunities and threats.

Competition -- Intraspecific competition (competition among individual bison) includes mate selection. Here, I view intraspecific competition as a mechanism responding to selective forces of the environment, not as a primary selective force itself; but that does not diminish its importance in bison evolution. Intraspecific competition is addressed in Chapter 5.

Interspecific competition (competition from other species) influenced where bison lived abundantly and where they were sparse or absent. The preponderance of the bison genome evolved in grassland environments where bison were most successful and abundant.

Rewilding Plains Bison

Bison were less successful in many other habitats, and we know little of their evolution and adaptation in those habitats. Such evolution would have led to regional diversity across the bison genome, and perhaps to sub-speciation of bison. Probably, such diversifying selection of bison was inhibited by two processes: continued or periodic genetic swamping of localized, small populations through interbreeding with larger populations from grassland habitats; and competition from other large herbivore species that had become specialists at living in habitats that would have been marginal for bison.

Interspecific competition involved more than bison competing for forage and other resources. Presence of other large mammals, as prey and as disease hosts, would have influenced the types and abundance of predators and disease organisms affecting bison. These factors would have influenced the ability of bison to persist and evolve in habitats and regions occupied by other species that were more adapted to those environments.

In the far north, including Beringia, bison shared late-Pleistocene environments with at least 13 other large mammal herbivores[1]. These were two kinds of horses, a camel, caribou, two kinds of moose, saiga, mountain goat, Dall sheep, two kinds of oxen, yak and the woolly mammoths. Fossils of mammoths, horses and bison are often found together from ice-age steppe habitats. Perhaps saiga, oxen and yak also competed in these habitats. Other species occupied habitats that were marginal, at best, for bison. Of the 13 species, 8 are extinct or disappeared from North America late during, or soon after, retreat of Wisconsin glaciers.

My purpose, however, is to focus on interspecific competition in the evolution of plains bison south of the ice sheets. During Wisconsin glaciation, bison shared this area with at least 32 other large mammal herbivores.[1] These included horses, a tapir, peccaries, camels and a llama, deer, caribou, moose, elk, several pronghorn species, mountain goats, bighorn, oxen, mastodons and mammoths. Of these 32 species, 23 disappeared from North America at or near the end of Wisconsin glaciation. Of the remaining 9, the musk ox is gone from the temperate zone, leaving only 8 species to compete with bison by about 10,000 years ago.

My interpretation is that, especially in the temperate zone, interspecific competition was important in keeping the vast majority of bison within steppe or grassland habitats. Thus, most bison evolution occurred in wide-open grasslands and bison are best adapted to these grasslands. However, most of this competition, constraining bison use of shrublands, mountain parklands, and open woodlands ended rather abruptly with extinctions of many species about 10-12,000 years ago. This allowed bison to expand their geographic range and to occupy many types of habitats (expand their ecological range) to encompass very much of what is now the contiguous United States and southern Canada.

Bison are not alone in this North American pattern of evolution and geographic and ecological expansion in response to the late Pleistocene extinctions of numerous large mammals. There were at least 39 species of large mammal herbivores in North America (32 south of the ice) near the end of Wisconsin glaciation. (Probably, there were several more. I have used a very conservative list, lumping much apparent variation into single species.) Diversity of large mammals in North America rivaled that seen today in Africa, where a long period of climatic stability has allowed diversifying evolution to produce very many species, many of which are habitat specialists.

Today, North America has only 12 species of large mammal herbivores. Only 3, white-tailed and mule deer and pronghorn, originated here. Eight species - elk, moose, caribou, bighorn and thinhorn sheep, musk ox, mountain goats and bison – are derived from rather recent (in geological time) immigrants from Asia across the Bering land bridge. Lastly, the peccary seems to have entered North America from the south after extinction of a larger North American peccary about 12,000 years ago.

Of the 12 existing North American large mammal herbivores, 7 had very large geographic and ecological ranges at the time of European contact. (Five of these are illustrated in Map 1.1). These were elk, caribou, moose, white-tailed deer, mule deer, pronghorn and of course, bison. While the geographic range of bighorn is comparatively small in area, it has a great longitudinal dimension, and bighorn exist in a variety of habitats. Only musk ox, thinhorn sheep and mountain goats have rather small geographic and ecological ranges. Collared peccaries have a large range in central and South America. Their expansion into the North American southwest following the Pleistocene extinctions fits the theory that relaxation of interspecific competition allowed most species to expand their geographic and ecological ranges rather recently.

Frequency distributions of the geographic ranges of existing large mammals, comparing Africa and North America (Charts 1.2, 1.3), support this argument. The "mature fauna" of Africa has very many species and a preponderance of species with smaller geographic and, therefore, smaller ecological ranges. In contrast, the depauperate, recently expanded North American large mammal fauna contains mostly species with large geographic ranges, each spanning many habitat types.

Two conclusions are: (1) The naturally-associated environment of plains bison is the Great Plains. This is the kind of environment in which most of their evolution occurred; the environment to which they are best adapted; where they are most productive and where they could be most easily restored and managed. (2) Plains bison can live in other environments. However, they are less well adapted to these habitats where they will be less productive and may require more careful management for restoration.

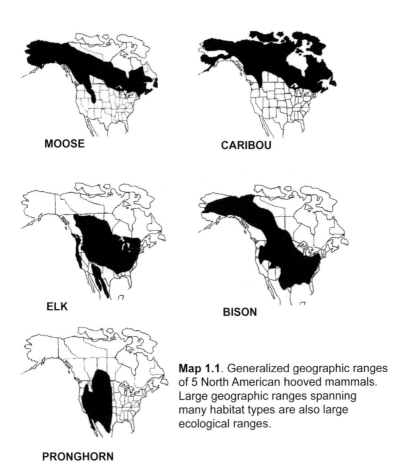

MOOSE

CARIBOU

ELK

BISON

PRONGHORN

Map 1.1. Generalized geographic ranges of 5 North American hooved mammals. Large geographic ranges spanning many habitat types are also large ecological ranges.

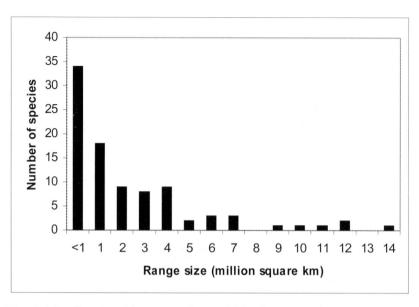

Chart 1.2. Geographic range sizes of 92 African hoofed mammals.

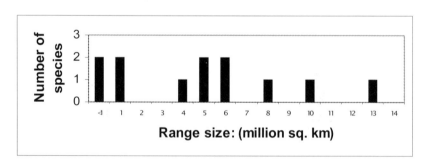

Chart 1.3. Geographic range sizes of 12 North American hoofed mammals.

From Steppe Bison to Plains Bison

Predation -- Northern predators of large mammals during Wisconsin glaciation included gray wolves, dhole (wolf-like canines), short-faced bears, grizzly and black bears, scimitar cats, American lions, and ice-age men[1]. Four of these eight predators disappeared during or shortly after the Wisconsin period. South of the ice, bison faced an even more formidable array of predators. At least 13 species of predators included gray wolves, dire wolves, dhole, short-faced bears, grizzly and black bears, sabertooth and scimitar cats, American lions, jaguar, cheetah, puma and men. Seven of these species disappeared from North America near the end of Wisconsin glaciation. Disappearance of several predator species likely was a factor allowing for expansion of geographic and ecological ranges of some large mammal herbivores, as discussed above.

Predation has been a major natural selective force that shaped bison of the past and present. Early bison faced a wide array of predator species, some of which were quite large, especially the short-faced bear that stood about 6 feet at the shoulders. There were ambush predators, such as American lions, and predators that ran and tested their prey, such as gray wolves. These large and powerful predators favored evolution of large, social bison with large, forward- or outward-curving horns as defensive weapons (Figs. 1.1, 1.2). Facing predators, bison could band together with their relatively defenseless calves at the rear.

However, the nature of predation as a selective force changed rather abruptly at the end of the Wisconsin period. Several large predator species disappeared and a new predator, man, arrived on the scene. Loss of predator species weakened selection for aggressive, large bison with defensive horns. Moreover, the new predator wielded and threw spears to safely overcome the defensive stance of bison. Thus, selection for very large defensive bison with large horns was weakened, and selection for bison that would escape by running fast and far became more important. (I have been told more than once that one might deter an overly threatening bison by throwing rocks at it. Do bison genes retain a memory that says, "Stay away from critters that throw things."?)

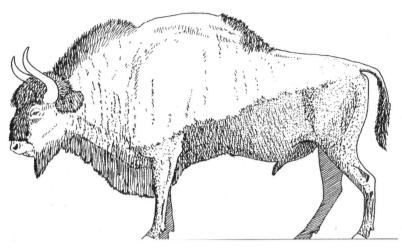

Fig. 1.1. Steppe bison, *Bison priscus*, was the first bison in North America, after crossing the ice-age land bridge from Asia (Courtesy, Valerius Geist).

Fig. 1.2 Steppe bison display at University of Alaska Museum. The model is based upon a 36,000-year old carcass preserved in permafrost (Courtesy, Dale Guthrie).

From Steppe Bison to Plains Bison

Wildlife biologists often refer to the "sanitation effect" of predation. This is the effect of predation, by removing more of the sick and more easily captured prey, in reducing the prevalence of disease in the prey environment. But, when predators have removed prey that exhibited disease symptoms, they were also selecting against strains of disease organisms that were most virulent toward their hosts. Thus, predators participated in the co-evolution of bison with their diseases. In the Yellowstone Park area of the United States, they still do.

Two more conclusions are: (1) Predation had a large impact on bison evolution. Yet, in the contiguous United States, only two herds in and near Yellowstone and Grand Teton Parks, live with effective predators today. Implications of this for the future of the wild bison genome are uncertain. Comparisons with the Yellowstone herd will be important and necessary for detecting and evaluating changes that will occur in most bison herds that lack effective predators. (2) Bison have co-evolved with year-round human predation. Hunting is not unnatural and should be the preferred and emphasized method for population control of some plains bison herds.

Disease -- Of the four primary selective forces that have given us today's bison, we know least about disease. The fossil record provides little evidence of past disease interactions of bison. While disease organisms are more diverse and abundant and evolve more rapidly in tropical climates, we cannot conclude that disease was unimportant during bison evolution in temperate and arctic climates. (Helminth parasites, perhaps 40,000 years old, have been found in frozen specimens of ice-age mammals from the far north.) What is important is that today's bison have retained robust physiological/anatomical mechanisms for disease resistance. There is no reason to conclude that bison cannot evolve with and adapt to the disease organisms they face today.

Disease organisms have also been evolving. Successful disease organisms do not quickly kill their hosts, nor do they debilitate their hosts such that predation occurs at an early age. Successful diseases tend to live with their hosts in ways that allow transmission of disease organisms to succeeding generations. Strains of the organism that kill or debilitate hosts in the presence of predators would fail. Natural selection tends to eliminate such strains of disease, producing an interspecies accommodation through simultaneous evolution of hosts and diseases in co-evolving systems that include predators and other threats working against the most lethal strains of diseases. For bison, wildness has always included this co-evolution.

Climate -- Extreme temperatures and precipitation, including drought and snow, have influenced bison evolution directly, and indirectly through impacts on quantity, quality, seasonality and availability of forage.

Much of bison evolution has occurred in a seasonally cold, relatively dry environment with seasonal vegetative growth. There was natural selection for bison that could gather and digest forage efficiently. These bison grew rapidly during each spring period of lush growth, which was prolonged in the arctic. Yet, during winter, bison could subsist on dormant, low quality forage hidden under a modest amount of snow. There was selection to retain body heat and to use energy efficiently. Thus, bison are a rather large mammal with a 4-part stomach, dense hair, and a hump, shoulders and feet designed for efficient travel over the hard substrate of dry grassland without deep snow. These adaptations are discussed further in Chapter 4.

Following Wisconsin glaciation, bison habitats became warmer and dryer, with shorter annual spring periods for lush vegetative growth. This trend was more pronounced in the temperate zone than in the arctic; and probably was most pronounced in the more southerly latitudes and during the post-glacial altithermal period of 5-9,000 years ago. The reduced forage quantity and quality would not support overly large bison. Big as they are, modern bison are smaller than their ice-age predecessors.

Prehistoric Bison

Much has been written of the prehistory of bison, including their evolution from even larger forms into the bison of today. I present but a brief overview of the more recent ice-age evolution of North American bison, based on interpretations of others who are more familiar with the fossil record.[2] The past of bison is incompletely understood, and probably always will be. The fossil record provides only a few pin-point glimpses of bison and their associated plants and animals, scattered across a multi-dimensional continuum of space, time and changing climatic and ecological conditions. For these and other reasons, all interpretations of bison evolution are somewhat speculation. Prudence requires that I present only major patterns that are generally, though not completely, accepted by today's authorities on bison evolution.

The steppe bison (*Bison priscus,*) was the earliest bison in North America, crossing the Bering land bridge from Asia about 200,000 or more years ago. We have stone-age drawings of steppe bison from caves in Europe and Asia. Much of what we know of this early bison is derived from analysis of an almost whole specimen, frozen in Alaska permafrost for 36,000 years.[3]

Steppe bison were larger than modern bison, had larger horns that curved forward, a thick mane over the shoulders, and a unique pelage-color pattern. They were clearly a different species (Figs. 1.1, 1.2, 1.3).

Steppe bison originated from cattle-like species in sub-tropical Asia long before the ice age. They evolved as specialized grazers in grassland habitats, first in temperate and later in arctic environments. They appear to have entered Beringia and North America during, or possibly before, Illinoian glaciation. Large size enhanced thermoregulation of Steppe bison in a cold climate, as the ratio of heat radiating surface area to heat generating body mass is lower in larger mammals. Large size, and large dangerous horns, also enhanced this bison's ability to gather and defend a bison group against the several large predators of Beringia.

Fig. 1.3 Steppe bison skull from 36,000-year old specimen, just removed from freezer for necropsy (Courtesy, Dale Guthrie).

Steppe bison penetrated the temperate zone of North America by Sangamon interglacial times (Chart 1). Presence of large predators favored evolution into very large, defensive bison. The extreme form was *Bison latifrons,* the giant bison that ranged largely south of the glaciated zone (Chart 1.1). Males of giant bison had horn spreads up to 7 feet. They were almost 50 percent larger than today's bison, and some stood over 8 feet tall at the shoulder (Fig. 1.4).

Fig. 1.4. A comparison of modern bison (left) and giant bison (*Bison latifrons*) bulls. Giant bison, late in the Pleistocene age, were up to 8 feet tall at the hump. (Courtesy, Valerius Geist)

Use of forage nutrients for growing large horns would have been most beneficial when (1) forage was relatively abundant, not limiting to horn growth; (2) horns had some defensive value against predators; and (3) large horns were a display signal and a weapon for demonstrating superiority in male competition for mates. All these conditions were present, especially during Sangamon interglacial times when giant bison flourished. Early in the Sangamon era, we expect bison populations were predator-limited, not forage-limited, fulfilling condition 1, above. Likewise, horns would have had defensive value for both males and females in a predator-limited population, fulfilling condition 2. Lastly, a relative abundance of forage allowed male bison to evolve efficient means for foraging and energy efficiencies that supported growth to large size with large horns in order for males to compete for breeding opportunities, fulfilling condition 3. Moreover, bison cows probably benefited by selecting large, dominant males for breeding, thus obtaining genes that produced a dominant male offspring, or an energy efficient female offspring, either of which favored perpetuating the cow's own genes.

The first relatives of modern bison appear in late Sangamon or early Wisconsin times (Chart 1.1). *Bison antiquus*, though smaller than *Bison latifrons*, was about 20% larger than today's bison, probably for the same reasons that *latifrons* was so large, noted above. The two species co-existed south of the Wisconsin ice, though giant bison were declining and may have persisted in outlying habitats as relict populations. As giant bison gradually disappeared during the Wisconsin era, *Bison antiquus* began its evolution, isolated by the ice from steppe bison in Beringia, into a smaller form of bison, especially in the southern regions. This evolutionary trend ultimately produced today's bison, *Bison bison*.

Meanwhile, during Wisconsin times, as Beringia reemerged with lowered sea levels, steppe bison were reunited with bison from Asia. Asian bison had already experienced predation from men. They may have adapted with an anatomy and behavior that emphasized escape rather than defense, and brought this evolved characteristic with them, initiating a trend in North American bison evolution that would accelerate when humans also reached the continent.

Extinctions of many North American large mammal species began late during Wisconsin glaciation and continued for a few thousand years after the ice receded. Several explanations for this mass extinction have been proposed, including over-exploitation by newly arriving human predators. The issue is still in doubt among scientists. Whatever the reason, steppe bison disappeared from the North about 10,000 years ago, along with horses, mammoths and many other species. In some regions, the demise of steppe bison may have been accelerated by competition or possibly by genetic swamping from more abundant bison that had evolved separately south of the ice and were recolonizing northward with glacial retreat.

South of the ice, in late Wisconsin and more recent times, evolution of bison into smaller forms would have been favored by five interrelated trends. (1) In a warming climate of late Wisconsin to recent time, the energy-conservation value of large body size was diminished. This warming and drying peaked during the altithermal period of about 5 – 9,000 years ago. (2) Disappearance of most large predators weakened selection for bison that were large, with large, forward or outward curving horns used in group defense. (3) Extinction of many predators allowed bison numbers to grow, creating forage competition and a forage limitation upon body size. (4) Forage quantity and quality declined, especially in more southern areas, as the climate warmed and dried, strengthening selection against larger bison with greater forage requirements. (5) Appearance of men, handling and throwing spears, reduced the survival value of a stand-and-defend strategy based on large size and dangerous horns (and favored a strategy based on escape through long-distance running). This scenario illustrates the complexity of natural selection as it operated on the bison genome, a process that continues today.

With receding Wisconsin ice, southern bison expanded northward at least as far as northeast British Columbia and north Alberta. They appear to have encountered descendants of steppe bison from the unglaciated Alaska-Yukon refugium that were expanding southward with the receding ice, but did not persist. Modern bison are mostly descendants of bison that evolved south of the Wisconsin ice. These diverged, perhaps 5,000 years ago, into two types, the wood bison in the north, and plains bison. (The nature and degree of this divergence continues to be a subject of much scientific debate[4] and does not concern us here.) Wood bison recolonized Alaska, the Yukon, Northwest Territories, and northern British Columbia and Alberta. Plains bison are slightly smaller and occupied territory below this line, into north-central Mexico (Map 2.1).

Thus, the bison lineage is long, diverse and magnificent. Today's bison carry the genetic heritage from steppe bison, giant bison and *Bison antiquus*. That heritage is a gift to us from thousands of years of evolution, with bison living, competing and dying. It is a gift we are using through domestication for commercial purposes. However, if we throw away most or all of the "wild part" of the bison genome, we will have lost the opportunity to view and hunt, and try to understand, truly wild bison that can continue to evolve and adapt to some remnants of wild America.

Footnotes:

[1]For a summary of Pleistocene mammals of North America, see Kurten and Anderson (1980).

[2] For more detailed and not always consistent discussions of *Bison* evolution in North America, see Dary (1974), Geist (1991, 1996), Guthrie (1990) and Gates et al. (2010). My brief and simplified review of North American bison evolution is intended primarily to emphasize the mechanisms, complexity and ages-old magnificence of the process.

[3] This frozen steppe bison, Blue Ox Babe, is described by Guthrie (1990). Guthrie's scholarly work has wide-ranging discussions of bison evolution and ecology.

[4] Gates et al. (2010) includes much discussion of current scientific opinions on the complex issue of Bison taxonomy, including the validity of *B. b. bison* (plains bison) vs. *B. b. athabascae* (wood bison) as separate subspecies. See Geist (1991, 1992 and Cronin et al. 2013) for the alternative opinion that wood and plains bison are not valid subspecies.

Chapter 2

Bison in Early Historical Time

The historical period is defined as beginning about 600 years ago, near the time of first European contact. Admittedly, this is drawing a line at a convenient place in the continuum of evolving bison in a changing North America.

Hernando Cortez likely was the first European to see bison – captive animals in Montezuma's zoo, far south of the natural range of wild bison. In about 1530, the shipwrecked Cabeza De Vaca, living among Native Americans along the Gulf of Mexico, perhaps in Texas, described and ate bison. In the 1540's, Coronado saw bison on the southern plains in his search for cities of gold.

The American perception of plains bison is based almost entirely on bison of the Great Plains. The history of bison east and west of the plains is not widely known or appreciated. As Europeans spread across the North American continent, bison were widely distributed east of the Mississippi, enormously abundant across the Great Plains, less abundant in the Rocky Mountains, and very scarce or absent from large areas west of the mountains (Map. 2.1).

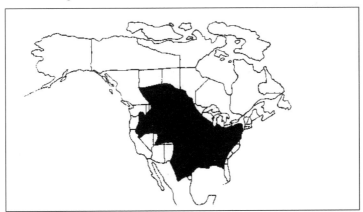

Map 2.1. Original range of plains bison in North America. The range of wood bison (not shown) occurred northward in Canada and Alaska.

This disparity was due to the relative qualities of bison habitats and to differences in incentives and opportunities for Native Americans, and later Europeans, for hunting and killing bison. The ability of hunters to limit and eliminate bison from a landscape depended upon the size of the bison population, its annual productivity, and its vulnerability to hunting. Bison obligated to using limited, patchily distributed habitats were more predictably located for killing. Hunters living among an abundance of alternative foods were more able to drive one food species, bison, to local extirpation.

(Sources for early geographic references to plains bison, below, are provided at the chapter end, organized by location. They are not foot-noted in the text.)

East of the Mississippi

Bison east of the Mississippi are mostly gone from the American memory. Yet they were once widespread and regionally abundant, leaving lasting impressions on the eastern landscape. There are towns named "Buffalo" in eight eastern states (Illinois, Kentucky, Minnesota, New York, Ohio, South Carolina, West Virginia, Wisconsin). There are "Buffalo Rivers" or "Buffalo Creeks" in at least seven states (Illinois, Minnesota, New York, Pennsylvania, Tennessee, West Virginia, Wisconsin) and "Buffalo Mountains" in four (Pennsylvania, Virginia, Tennessee, West Virginia). Several towns owe their names to ancient buffalo mineral licks or "stamping grounds". These include French Lick, Indiana and Stamping Grounds, Kentucky.

Bison occurred from New York to Florida and from the Mississippi River to the tide-water lands of the east coast. Locally, Native Americans, and later during the 17th and 18th centuries, Europeans depended upon bison for meat, shelter, clothing and other products. Well worn bison trails, called "traces" were commonly used for human travel, as they extended for many miles. Many became routes for today's roads and railroads. Buffalo traces were especially prominent leading to licks where bison dug and ate the soil to expose large areas of bare ground.

Early records of bison abundance, habitats and distribution are difficult to compare and interpret. In some places, bison may have been eliminated before they were described in writing. The earliest records are biased in emphasizing habitats along streams and rivers where humans traveled. Some accounts of bison abundance seem to be exaggerations and early records sometimes confuse bison with other big-game species. But there is no doubt: bison were once an important part of the eastern fauna.

Beginning in the 1670's, several Spanish journals record bison in Florida and neighboring southeastern states, especially in the Florida panhandle. While these bison were commonly hunted by Native Americans and Spaniards, and bison robes were common possessions, fewer than ten bison were recorded as being harvested in a day. Bison herds seem to have consisted of dozens, perhaps rarely a few hundred, animals.

Also during the 1670's, and into the 1700's, French explorers seeking furs and hides found bison plentiful in herds of a few to several hundred along the Mississippi and Illinois Rivers. Numerous French trading posts in the "Illinois Country" were based upon the productivity of that land, including bison. The town of Kaskaskia, Illinois reigned as a center for this trade. Feeding its population of several hundred European and Native peoples soon diminished the surrounding game. Bison were notably diminished near Kaskaskia by 1680.

The Illinois tall-grass prairies supported bison herds of at least hundreds of animals. This habitat extended across Indiana into Ohio and western Kentucky, becoming less predominant eastward. In 1769, Daniel Boone relates seeing buffalo numbering in the thousands on the western Kentucky bluegrass prairies. Such numbers were seen primarily at mineral licks that attracted bison from all directions, as evidenced by the numerous radiating traces. Also in 1769, George Washington killed bison in the Kanawha Valley of West Virginia. At this time bison were rather plentiful in the Ohio River

Valley. Soon, bison were part of a commercial trade, mostly of hides, along the Ohio River and its major tributaries, including the Wabash, Kentucky, Tennessee and Cumberland Rivers. Downstream, New Orleans became a shipping point for pelts to Europe and for salted meat to the West Indies to feed enslaved workers.

Bison appear to have been less abundant east of the Appalachian Mountains, and rare within the mountains. An Englishman first reported seeing bison near the Potomac River in 1612. Exploitation began almost immediately and bison were reported as scarce east of the mountains by 1750, and mostly gone by 1800. Aside from commercial hunters of meat and hides, early settlers relied upon wild game, including bison, to feed families until forest land could be cleared for domestic animals and crops.

Eastern bison were probably quite prolific in their moist region with productive vegetation. However, both Native Americans and Europeans killed bison in abundance. Native Americans were recorded using fire to round up bison for harvesting, and taking large numbers of animals. Bison were predictably located at licks, and probably along their traces. Often, most of a fallen carcass was wasted. Since bison and other game were originally abundant, hunters could take only the choicest parts, tongues, "hump meat" and marrow bones, with good prospects for taking another animal on the next day. Techniques for storing meat from so large an animal usually were not available. Meat did not dry easily in the moist eastern climate; and salt for curing was not always at hand.

Likely, Native Americans were limiting bison abundance and distribution in the East before 1500. Valerius Geist suggests that eastern bison must have increased in abundance and distribution during the 1600s when Native American tribes were decimated by epidemics of European diseases that spread from the coasts. Later, the arrival of Europeans inland, with the introduction of guns and the advent of commercial trade in hides and other bison parts, spelled doom for bison east of the Mississippi. Moreover, bison could not be tolerated amongst new agricultural fields, some of which were attractive forest openings for bison.

Bison in Early Historical Time

Extirpation of bison began in east Virginia tidelands in 1730, and proceeded westward. By the 1770s bison were gone from most or all of North and South Carolina, Alabama and Florida. Other terminal dates for bison are given as: Georgia in the early 1800s; Pennsylvania, 1801; Louisiana, 1803; Illinois and Ohio, 1808; Tennessee, 1823; West Virginia, 1825; Indiana, 1830; and Wisconsin, 1832.

Early records do not provide a comprehensive view of the habitat types that were important for eastern bison. Clearly, the tall-grass prairies of the middle Mississippi and Ohio River basins supported the most bison. Bison were also reported as frequenting "cane brakes". These tall grasses, related to bamboo, grew abundantly on the higher, better drained, portions of floodplains along southeastern rivers. Bison probably were not abundant within dense, continuous deciduous or coniferous forests, but seem to have used open forests and successional forest habitats, including the "flatwood" types near the Gulf coast, to some degree. However, the ecological distribution of eastern bison remains uncertain.

Fire was important in maintaining eastern bison habitat. Periodic fire is necessary to maintain tall-grass prairie, canebrakes, and open or successional forest habitat. Fires were both natural and man-caused. Native Americans used fire abundantly to manage their environment.

There probably were about 2-4 million bison east of the Mississippi. Very little remains of their once-primary habitats. Tall-grass prairies and canebrakes are now rare. These lands are some of the most subdivided, intensively used and productive agricultural lands in the nation. Opportunities for restoration of wild plains bison east of the Mississippi are slim, if they exist at all.

The Great Plains

The Great Plains were the naturally associated environment of plains bison. Habitat, including forage, was abundant and continuous. Consequently, bison herds were very large, productive and highly mobile. A bison herd exposed to a Native American hunting party could be a hundred or more miles away within hours of being attacked. Even after Native Americans obtained horses, they were not able to greatly diminish bison numbers over large areas of the plains. (However, the ability of Native Americans with horses, and later with guns, to diminish bison across the Great Plains was never fully tested.)

Most of the written history of plains bison, and most people's understanding of the abundance and annihilation of bison, are based upon early records from the Great Plains. Early explorers were astounded by the numbers of bison that sometimes stretched "as far as the eye could see."

Abundance

In 1804-1806, Lewis and Clark frequently referred to "innumerable" numbers of bison seen across a vast plain. In South Dakota, they noted at least 3,000 bison at a single glance. On their return trip, in 1806, they described, "without exaggeration", seeing a herd of 20,000 animals. In the same year, the Zebulon Pike expedition describes passing through an estimated 9,000 bison on a day's march along the Arkansas River. In 1820, the Long expedition reported (again with "no exaggeration") seeing at least 10,000 bison as part of a moving herd in Nebraska. In a rare winter observation, one herd of at least 126,000 bison was estimated near Wichita Kansas. Such numbers of bison lasted, at least locally, well into the 19th century. Referring to the period 1876-1882, buffalo hunter Vic Smith said, "10,000 buffalo might be seen at one look from any prominence" in the Yellowstone country of eastern Montana.

The large herds of bison were routinely described as accompanied by large numbers of wolves, sometimes in "bands of hundreds". We can only speculate on the movements and social relations of these wolves. Today, most wolves are territorial and comparatively sedentary. Did so many wolves follow bison over great distances, as some northern wolves follow migratory caribou today? If they did, when did the bison wolves stop moving long enough to den and produce pups? Perhaps plains bison were relatively sedentary during bison calving, allowing the wolves to reproduce. Caribou wolves in Canada and Alaska today produce pups during the caribou calving season.

Pristine plains bison herds covered huge expanses of territory. A large herd observed by the Pike expedition was estimated to extend 20 miles in width and 60 miles in length. In 1860, a buffalo hunter described "one continuous herd" of bison stretched along the Arkansas River for 200 miles. Also along the Arkansas, Colonel Dodge rode in 1871 for 25 miles through a herd along the river.

It has been suggested that such aggregations were largely a rutting-season phenomenon. However, several of the above observations occurred outside the bison rut - during May, June, September and December. Likely, such large aggregations of plains bison depended, not only on rutting behavior, but also on forage abundance and distribution and on attraction to water in dry times.

While these bison herds extended over vast areas, there were at any moment even larger areas with few or no bison. The large bison herds were mobile – here today and gone tomorrow. When the Long expedition saw a herd of over 10,000 bison one day, they awoke the next morning without a bison in sight.

Annihilation

In the Great Plains, the Native American nomadic culture based almost entirely on bison hunting and dependent upon horses was a short-term phenomenon, lasting about 150 years. Horses, reintroduced to the New World by the Spanish, reached the southern plains tribes around 1700 and the northern plains tribes in the 1730s. By the time of Lewis and Clark, nomadic bison-hunting tribes were well established. Crude estimates are that the annual take of bison, mostly prime-age females, was between 200,000 and 400,000. Given an annual take by predators and the periodic impacts of drought and of severe winters upon bison reproduction and survival, this take may have been depleting, at least in some years.

Rewilding Plains Bison

Local extermination of bison on the Great Plains began with Native Americans that lived in fixed villages based, at least partly, on agriculture. Lewis and Clark noted the rarity of bison surrounding the Mandan/Arikaree/Hidatsa villages on the upper Missouri. Along the eastern edge of the Plains, semi-agricultural tribes made annual or bi-annual hunts far into the Plains to access bison, suggesting they had annihilated bison closer to home.

However, the destruction of Great Plains bison really began with the Euro-American initiation of trade in bison robes, beginning around 1810. Native American harvest of bison for tradable robes was largely in addition to the take for subsistence purposes. The nomadic plainsmen were at a disadvantage in obtaining compensation for their bison robes. A nomadic lifestyle precludes owning large or heavy possessions. Thus, robes were traded for items that were either small or disposable, often beads, whiskey and cloth. This imbalance in trade negotiation produced huge profits for Euro-Americans that obtained trade goods inexpensively. The robe trade grew steadily.

In the eastern plains of Canada, early intensive robe-hunting began with the "Red River hunts", annual expeditions westward into the plains during 1820-1840. South of Canada, the robe trade depended largely upon Native Americans to harvest bison. Trade increased rapidly during the 1820s and 1830s, peaking in the 1840s. In 1825, 184,000 robes were shipped downriver and through New Orleans. Throughout the 1830s, the annual robe harvest in the USA is estimated to have been about 100,000. Isolated numbers of bison robes taken include 1835: 50,000 shipped down the Missouri River; 1840: 15,000 shipped over the Santa Fe Trail; 1849: traders at Fort Pierre collected 75,000 robes; 1850: 100,000 robes reached St. Louis; 1857: the upper Missouri River trade is estimated at 75,000 robes/year. Little is recorded of the continued bison harvest during the 1860s, especially during the Civil War; but it is clear that the slaughter continued. On the Missouri River, Fort Leavenworth processed 25-30,000 robes per year. Meanwhile, thousands of robes were transported annually from of the southern herd as well.

These numbers and speculations deny any demographic analysis.

However, it is clear that bison numbers were locally depleted during the robe trade. A decline of bison near Fort Union on the upper Missouri River was noted during the 1830s. In Canada, the Red River hunts were terminated after 1840 due to declining numbers of bison. An 1849 survey noted the relative lack of bison along the upper Missouri River, and eventual "exhaustion" of the resource was predicted. In the 1850s, the region east of Fort Pierre, South Dakota had been "hunted out" and bison were considered scarce in the eastern plains of Kansas and Nebraska. In 1863, one observer along the Arkansas River noted, "there was not a buffalo within 200 miles." Regional declines in bison numbers required shifts in traditional hunting grounds of Native Americans, with resulting increased inter-tribal warfare. Hostilities between invading Euro-Americans and Native Americans also increased.

Yet, very large numbers of bison persisted in large and distant grasslands. They would become the commercial resource for the ultimate near-annihilation of Great Plains bison in a fast and furious hunt for hides. In Europe and the eastern USA, industrialization produced a growing need for leather belts to run machinery. Once a technology for tanning bison hides developed, the fate of Great Plains bison was sealed.

Hide hunting differed in two important ways from the earlier robe trade. Robes were taken, mostly by Native Americans, during winter when bison coats were thick. In contrast, hide hunters were mostly Euro-Americans and they hunted year-round. While commercial profit was the driving force, destruction of the bison was cheered and abetted by the military as a means to subjugate Native Americans. The Army provided free ammunition and other supplies. Later, by 1880, the final bison destruction was applauded by a growing cattle industry that saw bison primarily as forage competition. As hide hunter Vic Smith put it, "The cattlemen wanted the buffalo exterminated, so the cattle could have the grass. As no one interfered, the white hunters slaughtered, indiscriminately, male, female and young."

The first center for the bison hide trade was Dodge City, Kansas, after the Santa Fe Railroad reached town in 1872. About 400,000 hides were shipped the next year (Fig. 2.1). Patient hunters using heavy Sharps rifles, accurate to several hundred yards, could take 50-100 bison per day. They employed skinners to peel and transport hides, leaving the rest of each carcass for the wolves or to decay on the prairie. By one estimate, over 1 million bison may have been slaughtered per year during 1872-1874, including crippling losses and other wastes.

Fig. 2.1. An estimated 250,000 bison hides piled for shipment from Dodge City, KS in 1874 (Kansas State Historical Society).

In 1874, Congress passed a bill to limit the bison slaughter, but President Grant refused to sign it.

In Kansas and Nebraska, the decimation of bison was so swift that hunters moved to Texas within a few years. The Texas harvest, mostly west and north of Abilene, may have peaked by 1876, and by

Bison in Early Historical Time

1877 most hide hunters had given up on west Texas. Perhaps only a few hundred bison remained from the great southern herd by 1880.

Hide hunting shifted northward in the 1880s. Bison were already "mostly gone" from the Dakotas and much of Wyoming. Real access to the Montana herds began with the arrival of the railroad at Miles City in 1881. One estimate puts 5000 hide hunters in Montana, Wyoming and the Dakotas in 1882. The railroad shipped 200,000 hides from an already depleted herd in that year, but only 40,000 in 1883 and but a few hundred in 1884.

The swiftness of the bison annihilation is astonishing. Almost all of the decisive hide hunting occurred within 15 years. In 1886, the chief taxidermist of the Smithsonian, William Hornaday, became so concerned over disappearance of plains bison that he mounted an expedition to collect a few of the last Montana animals for display at the National Museum. These animals are now in a museum in Fort Benton, Montana.

However, the final "clean-up" of Great Plains bison was accomplished by bone pickers. The abundance of carcasses scattered all across the grasslands fostered an industry based on bleached bison bones that were used in the East for sugar refining, in making buttons, tool handles and glue, and as fertilizer for the slightly acidic soils east of the Mississippi. Bone picking ranged from a family part-time business to those who concentrated on harvesting bones for a few years. In 1874, 32 million pounds of bison bones were shipped by rail from Kansas and Nebraska. By 1880, the southern plains were picked clean and bone hunting began in earnest on the northern plains with the arrival of the railroads.

Meanwhile, Native American nomads, devastated by European diseases, were being subjugated to reservations. Cattlemen were claiming the Great Plains, bringing with them strychnine for poisoning wolves. This practice also removed coyotes, swift foxes and other scavenging wildlife. Use of barbed wire began in the 1870s. Turf was plowed and some blew away. Prairie dogs, insects and unwanted plants were poisoned. Transformation of the wild Great Plains to a domestic environment was soon complete. The importance of bison as a pervading ecological force that had shaped the Plains ecology was, at the time, not recognized. Rapid disappearance of the magnificent, wild Great Plains that had coevolved over centuries was hardly noticed in the rush toward manifest destiny. Now the wind, the rain and the snow are all that remain, anywhere, of the vast wildness that was (Fig. 2.2).

Fig. 2.2. Buffalo, Oklahoma, on Buffalo Creek, has not seen a wild bison in many decades. Today, it is left to brag of other things.

The Rocky Mountains

In the Rockies, bison habitat was limited by forested cover and by climate, especially snow accumulation, at higher elevations. However, there is evidence of locally abundant bison in the intermountain valleys and bison also used alpine grasslands, above treeline, at least in summer.

Bison in Early Historical Time

Early writers described the mountain bison as smaller, more agile and blacker with longer, curlier coats, compared to their plains cousins. They were often described as more wary and as residing more in forested habitats, although these habits may have developed from decades of hunting that had already greatly reduced bison numbers. Early taxonomists argued for a separate sub-species to designate mountain bison. However, the present consensus is to consider all bison from south of central Canada as plains bison.

Numerous "buffalo jumps", used by Native Americans to kill and harvest bison in the Rockies of the northern states indicate that bison were once widespread within the mountains. Many of these jumps were used before 1500, and before Native Americans obtained horses. After 1700, horses were used in killing bison, in following bison across the landscape and for making periodic, perhaps seasonal, hunting trips to locations where bison could predictably be located. Records indicate that Native American hunting reduced bison and extirpated them from areas of the Rockies before major expeditions by Europeans produced written records of bison. Consequently, several mountain tribes made extensive annual or biannual hunts into the eastern Rockies and into the Great Plains to harvest bison.

In 1805-06, Lewis and Clark saw no bison in the Rocky Mountains, although in August, 1805, they recorded bison bones and excrement "of an old date" along the Jefferson River in Montana. Lack of bison observations in the Rockies during the well-known Lewis and Clark expedition is intriguing, but misleading. Likely, two factors limited the expedition's chances for seeing bison in the mountains. First, they traveled along the largest rivers; whereas mountain bison commonly migrated to higher elevations where forage was greener, at least in late summer. In this regard, trapper Osborne Russell noted that "Buffaloe are very particular in their choice of grass always preferring the short of the uplands to that of the luxuriant growth of the fertile alluvial bottoms." Second, after Lemhi Pass on the Montana/Idaho border, the expedition mostly followed well-traveled and presumably well-hunted Indian paths, and they were often near Native American villages. Probably, bison were eliminated from these areas, or they had learned to avoid them.

Whereas Lewis and Clark saw no bison along the Jefferson and Beaverhead Rivers in Montana, later observers recorded abundant bison in the vicinity. In the 1830's W. A. Ferris described the Jefferson River Valley south of Whitehall, Montana as "alive with buffalo". In 1840, Father De Smet noted that Native Americans killed more than 500 bison near the Three Forks of the Missouri (mouth of the Jefferson River). In the upper reaches of the Jefferson drainage, near the Lewis and Clark route, trapper Osborne Russell, in 1835, saw large numbers of buffalo scattered over the plains of the Ruby River Valley; and noted a valley full of buffalo near Red Rocks Lakes. Also in the 1830's, bison were reported using Horse Prairie west of Clark Canyon Reservoir, and near the Beaverhead formation along the river of the same name. In the 1840s, "Flathead" Indians from the Bitterroot Valley hunted long and extensively in southwest Montana and were able to find and kill up to 153 bison in a single day, as reported by Father Point who noted that the usual result of these hunts was "extermination" of the herd. West of this area, in Idaho, bison were reported in the Lemhi Valley by Peter Skene Ogden in 1825.

Further along the Lewis and Clark route, oral histories of Native Americans and observations of bison skulls indicated that bison had inhabited the Bitterroot Valley, probably into the early 1800s. To the east, along Clark's return route, both Clark in 1806 and De Smet in 1840 noted bison trails going over Bozeman Pass in Montana.

South of the Lewis and Clark route, Russell described "thousands of buffalo along Camas Creek near Du Bois, Idaho, and noted that "upwards of a thousand cows were killed" by a roaming Native village of 332 lodges and perhaps over 1900 individuals. The ratio of people to number of cows harvested suggests there was much waste of meat.

Bison were common in southeast Idaho and in adjacent Star Valley, Wyoming. Here, in 1834, Russell described "thousands of buffalo" along the Salt River and more thousands in the upper Snake River Plains northeast of Fort Hall. He also killed bison in this area in 1838, and upstream in Jackson Hole, Wyoming in 1836.

Eventually, wild bison persisted only in Yellowstone National Park. But this population was just an outlier of a larger population that had been extirpated. Early records indicate herds of a few to a few hundred bison in the Henrys Lake, Idaho, area and in the Madison, Gallatin and Yellowstone Valleys of Montana, near the Park. These bison likely intermingled with those at Red Rocks Lakes, southeast Idaho and in the Great Plains north of the Park.

In the Wyoming mountains, bison were common in the upper Green River drainage. In 1811, a party of "Astorians" noted bison as plentiful south of Union Pass. Near here, bison including "large bands" were noted near Pinedale, Wyoming at the mountain man rendezvous site on Horse Creek in 1835, 1837 and in 1838, though the latter rendezvous was held elsewhere. To the east, Joe Meek had noted there were plenty of buffalo near the 1829 rendezvous on the Popo Agie River near Lander. Further south, at the 1834 rendezvous on Ham's Fork near Granger, Wyoming, bison were described as abundant. Near here, Ferris had described "tranquil herds of buffalo in 1830.

In later years, bison skulls and bones have been found in the Snowy Range of the Medicine Bow Mountains, in Jackson Hole, along the Hoback River, in the Gros Ventre Mountains and in Yellowstone National Park.

In Colorado, Spanish explorers stampeded a herd of 500 bison in the San Luis Valley in about 1599. Bison were recorded in the Colorado Rockies by Zebulon Pike in 1807 and by John Fremont in 1844. Skeletal remains of bison have been found in and surrounding Rocky Mountain National Park, often above treeline. Locations include Estes Park, Horseshoe Park, Dunraven Meadows on the North Fork of the Thompson River, and Chambers Lake. In 1913, elderly Arapaho Indians recalled that bison ranged all through the mountain parks when they were boys.

Rewilding Plains Bison

Bison skulls have been exposed by a melting snowfield in Rocky Mountain National Park (personal communication, biologist David Stevens). The last bison in Colorado may have been killed in South Park around 1900, although Professor J. V. K. Wagar of Colorado State University told me that Colorado's last bison were in the Flat Tops area. On a 1980s elk hunt in the Flat Tops, my hunting partner found a bison horn imbedded in the soil of the Flat Tops.

This limited review of early observations of bison in the Rocky Mountains demonstrates that bison were once more common in the mountains than most Americans realize. They were numerous, at least at times, in the intermountain valleys, but also used parklands, open forests and some herds used alpine grasslands above the trees. While there were a few reports of herds of "thousands of buffalo" in the mountains, most reports indicate aggregations of much smaller numbers. Mountain bison herds seem to have been quite mobile, based on their trails crossing mountain passes and the adaptive mobility of Native Americans who hunted bison in the mountains. Bison mobility included altitudinal migrations to access the best available forages in any season.

The few bison surviving in Yellowstone National Park are the only plains bison to have survived continuously in the wild. Probably, there were fewer than 50 animals in 1902. The herd was eventually augmented with bison from northern Montana and from Texas. Thus, any unique genes of the original mountain bison in Yellowstone are now mixed with genes from two other sources. Today, two bison herds, in Yellowstone Park and in nearby Jackson Hole, are the only plains bison herds, on native range in the USA that live in wild conditions, including with effective predators.

The Far West

West of the continental divide, in the Great Basin and on the Columbia Plateau, bison were rare, and absent from vast areas at the time of European contact. Much of this land is dominated by shrubs adapted to arid conditions. In the Great Basin, productive habitats with grasses and sedges were patchily distributed. The arid climate limited forage production, in turn limiting the sizes and productivities of possible bison herds. Likely, bison would have been obligated to using local wetlands and riparian areas during most years. They would have been predictably located by hunters.

Bison were common in this area at the end of Wisconsin glaciation. They appear to have been extirpated from most or all the region during the prolonged altithermal period about 4,000 – 9,000 years ago and reestablishment did not fully occur until about 2,500 years ago. They flourished for a time, becoming quite rare again by about 1500 AD at the end of a more moist climatic period. Climate, with its effects on forage abundance, quality and distribution no doubt played an important role in causing these fluctuations. However, predation by Native Americans attacking small, less productive herds, probably in limited, predictable habitats, may also have been involved.

With alternative food resources, Native Americans could have maintained their own numbers while they decimated and extirpated local big-game herds. On much of the Columbia Plateau, the alternative prey were salmon. This relationship may have contributed to the rarity or lack of late-prehistoric or historic records of bison in the lower Snake River drainage.

A result of the interaction of environment and Native American hunting is that there are few historical records of bison across large areas of what is still considered native bison range. Lewis and Clark never saw bison along the Columbia River in 1805-6. In 1827, Jedediah Smith crossed the Great Basin, west to east, without seeing bison, although Native Americans told him there were bison "a few days" to the northeast, probably in the Snake River drainage. In 1832, Milton Sublette and Joe Meek, hunting in northern Nevada between the Humboldt and Owyhee Rivers, found no game in a "barren country". However, Hornaday's 1889 map includes this area as original bison range.

Early records suggest there were at least a few bison north of the Great Salt Lake, and still more east of the Lake. In 1829, Peter Skene

Rewilding Plains Bison

Ogden, within distant sight of the Great Salt Lake, and probably to its north, noted abundant bison sign. In 1833, Bonneville's beaver trappers killed a bison near the north side of the Lake. Eastward, Osborne Russell noted that there had been bison along the Wasatch Front near Utah and Great Salt Lakes, but that they were long gone by the 1840s. There are fossil records from bison in this area during about 1400-1700 AD.

Based on fossil evidence, there was a center of bison occupation in southeast Oregon, in the Malheur Lake country, after 1500 until possibly as late as 1800. According to Native American oral traditions, these bison occasionally roamed into northeast California and extreme northwest Nevada. Few in numbers, most did not persist in the face of Native American harvesting. In the very early 1900s, some older Natives believed that a small detached band of bison once lived permanently northwest of where Susanville California is now located.

However, there is much archeological evidence of bison in the northern Great Basin and on the Columbia Plateau. Some of this evidence indicates bison were present in some locales until a few centuries before European contact. More than 50 archeological sites from southeast Washington contained evidence of bison in association with human artifacts. There are at least 5 such sites in northern Nevada, especially in the Humboldt River Drainage. Most or all of these sites date from at least 600 years ago, a time when the Great Basin was more moist than today, and would have provided more and better forage to support bison in numbers able to persist with pedestrian human predation.

We should not conclude that these areas in the Great Basin and on the Columbia Plateau cannot support bison today. I believe large areas in northern Nevada, southeast Oregon and perhaps southeast Washington, where domestic cattle now roam, could support meaningful numbers of wild plains bison.

Bison in Early Historical Time

*   *   *   *

Attempts to define the "original" or "pristine" range of bison are bedeviled by the sometimes perceived need to select a point in time to represent the distribution of the species. However, bison distribution has been dynamic, fluctuating with changing climate conditions and impacted by Native American predation before European contact. Moreover, selecting any narrow point along the timeline will limit the number of observations available as a basis for representing the bison range.

Map 2.1 represents the former range within which plains bison distribution fluctuated during late pre-historic through early historic times. It is a period when climates and vegetation were at least similar to those of today. Wild bison can survive throughout this former range. Restoration of bison is appropriate in some areas, especially in the Far West, even though bison were absent from these areas at the time of European contact.

Few Americans are aware that plains bison once occurred in at least 40 of the 48 contiguous United States, including 33 where bison roamed over major portions of the states. The Endangered Species Act allows for listing a species as threatened or endangered if the species is in trouble throughout a significant portion of its range. Clearly, wild plains bison are gone today from a significant portion, probably more than 99%, of their former range. But that is a subject for a later chapter.

The history of plains bison does not end here. There is much to tell of bison in the 20th century. This is covered in Part III. But first, I must address complex and sometimes technical aspects of wild bison. A review of the status of bison, largely under captivity since 1900, will be more meaningful with a background on what constitutes "wildness" in bison and how extinction still threatens wild plains bison.

References:

Early records of bison were extracted for the following regions:

East of the Mississippi: I relied upon Belue (1996). One reference is to Geist (1996).

Great Plains: The 18th and 19th century history of bison has been reviewed and described many times. I relied upon:

Biddle (1814), Burroughs (1961), Dary (1974), DeVoto (1953), Evans (1997), Gard (1959), Geist (1996), Isenberg (2000), Lott (2002), Smith (1997), Shaw and Lee (1997) and Zontek (2007).

Rocky Mountains: Early records of bison in the Rocky Mountains are diverse and scattered. Dary (1974) notes early descriptions of mountain bison as being different from those of the plains. On habits and ecological relations of bison in the mountains, see Hasselstrom (1984).

Montana: Burroughs (1961), Donnelly (1967), Carriker, R. C. (1995), Fryxell (1928), Haines (1965), Meagher (1973), Phillips (1940). Records of bison in western Montana are reviewed by Adams and Dood (2011). However their account of 150 bison killed in 1842 near Missoula seems to be an inaccurate interpretation of Father Point, in Donnelly (1967).

Idaho: Hafen (1965) reference to W. A. Ferris, Haines (1965),

Wyoming: Fryxell (1928), Gowans (1985), Haines (1965), Lavender (1985). Meagher (1973), Vestal (1952),

Colorado: Dary (1974), Fryxell (1928); the reference to bison in the San Luis Valley is from the Nature Conservancy, but I have not been able to trace the source.

Far West

The Great Basin/Columbia Plateau: Daubenmire (1985), Grayson (2006), Van Vuren (1987),

Bison in Early Historical Time

<u>Utah</u>: Grayson (206), Hafen (1965), Haines (1965),

<u>Idaho</u>: Butler (1978),

<u>Nevada</u>: Van Vuren and Dietz (1993), Vestal (1952),

<u>Oregon</u>: Van Vuren and Bray (1985).

<u>Washington</u>: Grayson (2006), Lyman (2004),

<u>California</u>: Merriam (1926),

Part II

The Dimensions of Wildness

Given that all the wondrous animals of the world are bequethed to us by natural selection, why would we choose to weaken or replace natural selection at every possible opportunity?

Chapter 3

Extinction

Plains bison are not extinct. But what is extinction and how will we know if and when it has occurred? To answer, we must address the characteristics and processes of extinction.

When we think of extinction, we are reminded of passenger pigeons, Carolina parakeets and heath hens. They are all gone. North American bison barely escaped numerical extinction in the late 19th century. There were fewer than two hundred plains bison left. We tend to think of extinction solely in quantitative terms. A species is extinct when none remain. A species is in danger of extinction when few remain. However, there is more to the process of endangerment and extinction than a simple decline in numbers. Aspects of the complex extinction process are described briefly here, with elaboration in later chapters.

Numerical Extinction

Numerical extinction involves a decline in numbers, sizes and distributions of species populations, and declining exchange of animals and genes among populations.

The wildlife profession seldom recognizes the loss and fragmentation of megapopulations of wildlife that once generated and maintained more genetic diversity than we have the capacity to retain today. Rather, for many species, management has degenerated into efforts to maintain minimum populations necessary for short-term viability.

Clearly, there once was a megapopulation of bison on the Great Plains. To the east and west, bison herds must have been smaller and more scattered, with less exchange of animals and genes among them. Large, but somewhat isolated, herds of plains bison east of the Mississippi River and west of the Rocky Mountains would have had the best opportunities to evolve and adapt to local environments. This process would have diversified the overall gene pool of plains bison. However, as local herds declined and became more isolated they would have lost genetic diversity and chance events affecting survival and reproduction could have overwhelmed natural selection. Local adaptation must have ceased.

Some large populations of bison probably existed with many subgroups that exchanged individuals and genes. Populations structured in this way are called "metapopulations". The flow of individuals and genes between two subpopulations is not always equal in both directions. When one subpopulation is small, the flow of animals can be entirely in one direction.

Smaller, more isolated herds of bison will lose genetic diversity and will have a greater probability of extinction. In a small herd within a metapopulation, these negative trends are offset by the in-migration of animals and their genes. The processes are called "demographic support" and "genetic support", wherein the persistence and genetic diversity of a small herd are supported by contributions from a connected larger population.

So the trend of numerical extinction is more than a simple decline in the number of animals. Along the way, large herds become smaller and connected herds become more isolated. Eventually, it becomes a self-generating process as small, isolated herds become inbred, lose genetic diversity and their ability to adapt to changes and challenges of their environments. Further, chance events are more likely to cause extinction of smaller and more isolated populations. Small populations tend to become even smaller, until they are gone.

Ecological Extinction

A species is ecologically extinct when it no longer exists in the wild, interacting in age-old ways with soils, plants and other animals in a natural ecosystem. Plains bison are gone from about 99 percent of their original range. They are ecologically extinct over an even greater proportion of that range. The most obvious ecological effects of plains bison on prairie ecosystems include: [1]

•	Grazing, trampling, wallowing and nutrient recycling enhance diversity of the vegetation, affecting the height, density, species composition and productivity of the flora in patches of a few square yards to at least many acres.

• Bison redistribute and concentrate nutrients in the environment, with urine and feces, and especially where bison die.

• Wallowing and trampling, with impacts on vegetation, influence hydrological processes, and the distribution of water on the landscape. Once, large areas with about 10 wallows per acre were common. Ephemeral ponds in bison wallows provided reproduction habitat for frogs and toads.

• Bison transport plant seeds, in their hair and in food/feces. This is especially important for annual plant species that must frequently reestablish themselves on recently disturbed, temporary habitats.

• Bison dung enhances several dung dependent insects, including some ant species and dung beetles. Interactions of dung dependent insects and fungi in grassland, or other, ecosystems are little understood.

• Through effects on the vegetation and soils, bison alter fuel loads and natural fire regimes, influencing the frequency and intensity of fire and the sizes of burned areas. Fire has many cascading effects on other plants and animals.

• Impacts on vegetation and soils create patterns of nesting, hiding, feeding and travel habitats for other species, including pronghorn antelope, prairie dogs, badgers, foxes, grassland birds, mice and voles, snakes, amphibians and insects. These species, in turn, affect still other species, especially their predators and prey, in cascading effects.

• Bison provide forage competition for elk and perhaps other wild grazers.

• In areas with much snow, bison expose forage used especially by following pronghorn antelope and deer. Bison also create trails that are used by several other herbivorous and carnivorous mammals. Even birds forage and shelter within bison feeding craters in snow.

Rewilding Plains Bison

- As prey, and as carcasses, bison provide for predators and scavengers. The ecosystem value of a bison carcass is extended by harboring many insect species that are food for small avian and mammalian insectivores that are, in turn, prey of larger predators. Lastly, bison bones provide a concentrated source of calcium and other minerals sought by many gnawing mammals.

- Through rubbing and other physical effects, bison reduce or destroy woody vegetation, inhibiting woody invasion of prairies.

- In annual shedding, bison provide insulating and water repellent wool that is used effectively by small mammals and song birds as nesting material. One study suggests that nests with bison wool suffer less predation because bison hair masks odors of the nest site. [2]

The original ecological role of plains bison in the eastern third of our country may never be known. We have inadequate records of habitat use, grazing habits and seasonal movements of these bison. They were gone before they could be recorded.

Most of our knowledge of the ecosystem relations of bison comes from the Great Plains. On these plains, impacts of bison, interacting with fire, drought, topography and weather, upon the grasslands were enormous as bison moved over vast distances creating various sized patches of diverse vegetation. Probably, some areas were ungrazed for years or longer. Other areas, heavily grazed during one visit by a large bison herd, may not have been grazed again for years. Today in the USA, no area where bison might be restored in the Great Plains is large enough to fully recreate this pattern and process.

West of the Plains, we have little knowledge of the original ecology of bison in the Rocky Mountains and almost nothing is known about bison west of the mountains. Early trappers left scant information on habitat use by bison in the mountains. There is no information on annual and seasonal movements of these bison. West of the mountains, there were almost no bison to observe as they had been eliminated almost everywhere by Native American hunters.

In nearly all of the few places where plains bison remain, their once large ecological influence as a very mobile grazer is, at best, minimized. Species of plants and animals that evolved with plains bison are diminished because their evolution best fitted them to an environment that no longer exists.

Our Endangered Species Act recognizes the threat of ecological extinction. A purpose of the Act is to conserve the ecosystems upon which threatened and endangered species depend. This recognizes the dependence of a species upon its ecosystem. But the Act does not clearly recognize the dependence of an ecosystem upon the species. The concept of declining numbers of populations and individuals of a species is easy to grasp. The complexities of ecological relationships among soils, plants and animals are not. Consequently, the threat of ecological extinction has not been a major consideration in listing decisions under the Endangered Species Act.

Genetic Extinction

Genetic extinction occurs when a species evolves into a new form. It is the most gradual, least obvious and most insidious process of extinction. With genetic extinction, we still have animals, but they are different animals. Some would argue that genetic extinction is simply evolution in action. However, when the genetic composition of a population changes, with significant reduction or permanent loss of genes that best fit animals for survival and reproduction in a wild environment, "wildness" of the population is diminished. At some point, we must consider the wild form to be extinct.

Genetic extinction of the wild bison genotype has been occurring through five processes. These are (1) initiating herds with few individuals (founders) having limited genetic diversity, (2) crossbreeding with cattle genes, (3) inbreeding in small herds, (4) genetic drift in small populations, and (5) artificial selection by human intervention resulting in genotypic adaptation to a captive or semi-captive environment (domestication). All these processes, synergistically, weaken or replace natural selection in bison herds.

Rewilding Plains Bison

Founder Effects

At the continental level, much genetic diversity must have been lost in reducing plains bison from perhaps 30 million animals to fewer than 200. At the local level, many of today's herds have been initiated with very few bison, providing small samples from that already limited genetic diversity. Ultimately, the potential for effective natural selection has been reduced.

Genetic Introgression

Early attempts to save bison from extinction routinely involved some crossbreeding with cattle. Often the process was intentional. Cattlemen desired to combine the hardiness of bison with the meat-producing characteristics of cattle. It is also likely that some unintended crossbreeding occurred simply because a few bison were kept with cattle.[3]

Attempts to produce "beefalo" or "cattalo" were largely failures. Cattle bulls are reluctant to mate with female bison. Bison bulls are more accommodating. However, the result is often fatal for both the beef cow and the offspring. All first-generation hybrids have low fertility, with male offspring usually being sterile. But a few hybrids survived, and were bred back into the bison herds. Through subsequent breeding among bison, cattle genes spread.

As a result, most plains bison and most plains bison herds now contain cattle genes. Every bison has not been examined, and the entire genome has not been examined for any bison. However, genetic analyses to date suggest that fewer than 8000 plains bison in North America are free of cattle genes.

Cattle-gene introgression has produced some obviously strange looking animals, such as a bison with white faces. However, most plains bison have small amounts of cattle genes and the results are not readily apparent in the anatomies of the animals. One study found that bison with the most cattle-gene introgression tend to be smaller at an early age and never grow so large as more pure bison.[4] Effects of cattle-gene introgression upon behavioral and physiological traits of bison have not been studied.

There may be only 2 substantial plains bison herds in the United States that are entirely free of cattle genes. These are the Yellowstone National Park bison and a private herd in New Mexico belonging to Ted Turner Enterprises. The Turner herd originated with animals from Yellowstone. In Montana, the American Prairie Reserve is developing a herd of pure bison, largely by obtaining animals from a pure herd in Canada. This herd, now 200 bison, will be grown to a substantial size.

A bison herd at Wind Cave National Park, originating with Yellowstone animals, was long considered free of cattle introgression. Recently, cattle genes have been found in this herd, probably due to breeding with cattle-introgressed bison from the adjacent Custer State Park. One small bison herd in the Henry Mountains of Utah may also be free of cattle genes. Again, this herd was founded with Yellowstone bison.

Inbreeding

Breeding of closely-related individuals occurs in small herds, or in herds maintained with few bulls. Likely, there are behavioral tendencies in bison to avoid inbreeding when possible. But we know little of this, and nothing of the effectiveness of outbreeding behavior in small herds. Negative effects of inbreeding on reproduction and survival (Chapter 5) replace natural selection in determining the future genetic makeup of the herd.

Genetic Drift

Genetic drift is discussed in Chapter 5. Genetic drift occurs when random chance determines which genes or animals survive and reproduce, causing genetic change in a population. In very large populations, random events affecting transmission or survival of genes are relatively unimportant. Beneficial and deleterious genes are affected almost equally. This leaves abundant opportunity for natural selection to operate, favoring beneficial genes and purging deleterious genes from the population.

However, in small populations, genetic drift may cause some genes to disappear, reducing genetic diversity and evolutionary potential. Further, genetic drift may weaken or overwhelm natural selection as random events predominate in determining the success or failure of genes. The genetic composition of the population "drifts away" from being highly adapted to the local environment. The result is genetically different animals.

Artificial Selection and Domestication

Domestication, a major threat to persistence of wild plains bison, is discussed in more detail in Chapter 8. It is most pronounced in private, commercial herds that contain a large majority of remaining plains bison. However, public bison herds and private herds owned by conservation organizations are also subjected to practices that lead toward domestication. Currently, even the Yellowstone Park bison herd is affected by domesticating activities.

Domestication results from the replacement or weakening of natural selection by artificial, human-managed selection. Intensive management of bison can result in rapid, though not obvious, genetic changes and loss of adaptations to the wild environment.

Summary

Processes discussed briefly above are summarized in Fig. 3.1. As the reader plows through the more detailed discussions of these processes in later chapters, it will be useful to refer back to Fig. 3.1, to place each process in context with other processes of the complex progression toward extinction.

The key element of habitat loss is missing in Fig. 3.1. By their nature, wild bison require large areas of diverse habitat. They will not continue to be wild bison without it. Loss of this bison habitat has occurred as more and more land, public and private, has been dedicated to other purposes, especially to livestock production. Unlike most endangered species, bison numbers and distribution were not originally diminished by loss of habitat. Bison were reduced

Extinction

largely for commercial and military/political purposes. The habitat of plains bison became intensively used for other purposes, mostly after bison were gone. However, restoration of wild plains bison will require rededication of at least a few large areas of diverse, public land to native grassland with bison.

Extinction is a serious matter. Numerical extinction of a species deprives future generations of any opportunity to use, enjoy, study, and be inspired by the animals. Ecological and genetic extinctions offer little less deprivation. Ecological extinction removes important ecological relationships of bison from a grassland ecosystem. Other species of plants and animals are diminished in cascading effects. Future generations are deprived of the values of these naturally functioning ecosystems. Genetic extinction will gradually remove the hardy, efficient, disease-resistant, alert, agile, awe-inspiring animal - the truly wild bison of our history and legends. It is not bison, but the bison genome that we pass to future generations. We owe it to our grandchildren to create a place where we may bequeath them wild plains bison.

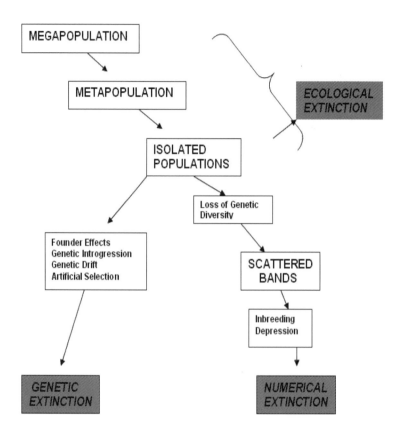

Fig. 3.1. Summary of processes leading toward three forms of extinction of wild plains bison on native range in the USA.

Footnotes

[1] Gates et al. (2010) and Knapp et al. (1999) review the ecological role of plains bison as a keystone species affecting plants, other animals, soils and hydrology of grassland habitats. Fuhlendorf et al.

(2010) compare and discuss some differences between the ecological relations of bison vs. domestic cattle under managed conditions.

[2] Coppedge (2009, 2010) describes use of bison hair as nesting material by grassland birds.

[3] Reviews of the problem of cattle-gene introgression in bison are in Freese et al. (2007) and Hedrick (2009). Freese et al. concluded that 98.5% of plains bison now have some cattle genes. However, the proportion of cattle genes in each bison is estimated as usually being <2% (Hedrick 2009). At the 2011 American Bison Society meeting in Tulsa, Oklahoma, geneticists concluded that issues of genetic purity of bison should be of less concern than forward-looking concerns for management issues such as restoring natural selection.

[4] Derr et al. (2012).

Chapter 4
Wild Bison

Wild bison are wondrous, awe-inspiring beasts. Seeing them in winter arouses visions of large bison evolving with mammoths and dangerous short-faced bears on Beringian steppes. Viewing them in summer invokes images of nomadic Native Americans, truly free peoples, traveling unrestricted across the vast Great Plains, following bison. But what is the nature of wildness in bison? What characteristics of wildness are at stake through domestication? To answer such questions, we must consider some esoteric details of wild bison.

Evolution and fitness

Wild animals are products of their past evolution in wild environments. In large populations, where chance events such as unusual mortalities have affected only a small proportion of the animals, natural selection has been the main mechanism of evolution. Natural selection operates when characteristics of the environment determine which animals survive and reproduce, leaving their genes in succeeding generations. For bison, major factors of natural selection likely have been predation, competition for resources, especially for forage and, among bulls, for mates, disease, and severe weather, sometimes in combination with limited forage or limited water resources. Genes that are expressed as traits being favorable responses to these factors will survive and increase in the population. Bison without these genes and traits are less successful at survival and reproduction and leave relatively few of their genes in the next generation.

Thus, it is characteristics of the environment that "select" which animals are successful and which genes persist. An animal, or group of animals, whose genetic traits favor survival and reproduction is said to possess a high degree of "fitness". Fitness may be measured by survival and reproduction or by the proportion of an animal's genes that persist in the genetics of succeeding generations. But to an ecologist, "fitness" refers to the degree to which the animal or population is "fitted", by evolution, to its recent environment. Recognizing that fitness is the result of an evolutionary process, "fitted" becomes a synonym for "adapted". In this sense, favorable genetic traits are "adaptations" to an environment.

Bison as an adaptive syndrome

Each bison is a bundle of adaptations - characteristics that have successfully persisted with natural selection. There are adaptations to the physical, biotic and social environments. Natural selection has occurred in changing environments and diverse locations. What we have left of the bison genome today reflects the temporal, spatial and ecological diversity of natural selection in former bison habitats.

Adaptations are often classified as anatomical, physiological or behavioral.

While it is convenient to discuss adaptations as separate characteristics of animals, they are interdependent and can not exist separately. An herbivore's adaptations for foraging and nutrition will involve the type and size of its digestive tract, the anatomy of its mouth and teeth, its digestive enzymes, and its food habits. In addition, the animal's foraging behavior must be consistent with its social behavior in terms of forage competition and with its methods for detecting and evading predators while feeding. Thus, an adaptive syndrome is the set of coordinated anatomical, physiological and behavioral adaptations that fit the animal to operate in certain ways in a limited array of environments. Wild bison are a unique adaptive syndrome reflecting their past evolution.

It is common to speak of adaptations as the "strategy" of a species, as if evolution were a conscious process of solving the problems of living and reproducing in an environment full of potential resources and enemies. We may speak of bison as having "solved" nutritional and survival problems in an environment with only seasonal forage abundance, a severe climate, and voracious predators. Learned behaviors may be adaptations reflecting conscious decisions of individual animals. But most of what is a bison is not learned; it is genetic in origin. Even learned behaviors must depend upon the animal's genetic adaptations for implementation. We recognize that natural selection for suitable adaptations has come slowly with a cost of very many dead or non-reproducing animals. Adapting through natural selection is a slow and costly process.

As responses to past environments, some adaptations of bison may not be expressed, or may be useless, in today's environments. Thus the bison ability to move great distances in response to forage conditions, weather, availability of water, or predators will not be expressed in almost all bison ranges today. Most bison ranges are too small. Many are subdivided by fences into smaller, seasonally used pastures. In this way, as we restrict the environment of a wild animal, we may never see all that the animal really is. Moreover, adaptations in the genome that are no longer beneficial may not be retained.

Our understanding of the anatomical, physiological and behavioral adaptations of bison is very incomplete. However, it is useful to consider some of what we know of bison. Otherwise we will fail to recognize the complexity and full dimension of unique attributes, known and unknown, that we risk losing through domestication. Following is a glimpse of the adaptive syndrome that is bison. [1]

Adaptations to the Physical Environment

Bison are extremely tolerant to cold. Their large size provides the thermal advantage of a relatively low ratio of surface area to body mass. (Note that a 1-inch cube has a surface/mass ratio of 6:1, that is 6 sq. in. per 1 cu. in.; whereas a 2-inch cube has a surface/mass ratio of only 3/1, 24 sq. in. per 8 cu. in.) While body mass generates heat, surface area facilitates heat loss. Thus, large size is an advantage for maintaining body temperature in a cold environment. Small external ears, thick necks and relatively short, stocky legs further limit a bison's surface area.

Winter is a season of nutritional stress for northern grazing animals. Forage is less abundant and less available under ice and snow. However, bison adapt by lowering their metabolic rates[2], requiring less energy and forage, at this season.

The large bison rumen, the "vat" wherein symbiotic bacteria digest fibrous forages, is also a heat source. Digestion produces heat that maintains body temperature.

Bison fur is exceptional insulation. I am told it is 10 times as dense as cattle hair.[2] In cold conditions, snow may accumulate on a bison's insulated back without melting (Fig. 4.1). Bison hair is longer in the cape on the front half of the animal than on the rear. This allows bison to face into the wind during a cold storm. In summer, less hair over the rear of a bison may also allow for some dissipation of "excess" heat produced by the rumen.

Fig. 4.1. The lower critical temperature of a bison is about minus 40 degrees. (Don MacCarter photo).

With these and no doubt many more, adaptations to cold, the bison's lower critical temperature – at which it must increase its metabolism to maintain body temperature – is about minus 40 degrees! [3]

Bison are adapted for handling a modest amount of snow. Using their powerful necks and heads with dense fur, they are able to push aside snow to access forage. They can plow through deep snow, and the habit of traveling single-file minimizes energy expenditures, at least for the following animals. During winter, they repeatedly use the same trails, minimizing energy costs.

While grown bison are well adapted to cold and the season of limited forage, their young calves are more vulnerable. It is therefore advantageous for bison calving to be well timed in the spring to optimize calf survival. Calves born at the best time will nurse from cows that may access the best spring flush of forage, providing maximum quantity and quality of milk. These calves begin weaning and foraging on their own during summer while some forage is yet green. They can maximize growth, enhancing chances for surviving their first winter as small, subordinate animals in a competing herd. Early-born calves may succumb to a late-winter storm. Late-born calves may not survive the following winter. As noted below, predation may augment this selection by favoring synchronous birthing among bison cows. Thus, natural selection operates to favor bison with genes that produce well-timed breeding and birthing seasons.

Artificial feeding of bison may subvert this natural selection. With winter feeding, as in the Jackson, Wyoming bison herd, late-born calves may not be eliminated by forage deprivation in winter. Very young, red calves have been seen in the Jackson bison feed lines in December, and some have survived the winter.[4]

Adaptations to the Biotic Environment

The challenges of a wild animal are to find, compete for and use resources; and to avoid, escape and defend against enemies. For wild bison, this largely involves a foraging strategy, disease resistance, and a predator defense/evasion strategy.

<u>Foraging Strategy</u>

An average adult bison will consume about 30 pounds of forage daily. In general, forages of higher quality, being more easily digested and containing higher levels of protein and other nutrients, produce larger, faster growing, healthier animals that are more active and more fecund. However, the highest quality forages, such as the leaves of forbs, flowers, buds and seeds, are relatively rare and dispersed in nature. In contrast, lower quality, less digestible forages, such as grasses and sedges, are more abundant and densely distributed, allowing for rapid harvest. Thus, grazing mammals face a tradeoff between obtaining forage quality and acquiring forage quantity.

Smaller mammals, with less demand for daily food intake, have time to emphasize the seeking of dispersed higher quality forages. In turn, these forages tend to be relatively easy to digest. A large digestion apparatus -- not possible in a small animal -- is not needed. Pronghorn and deer, for example, require only 3-5 pounds of forage per day. They forage at a leisurely pace, often moving between bites and interrupting foraging to scan their environment.

Being very large mammals with large forage requirements, bison are obligated to feeding mostly upon the more abundant but lower quality forages. Their large daily energy requirement does not allow spending time to seek and find the best, but more dispersed forages. Bison must forage in habitats where forages are abundant and densely distributed for easy and rapid harvest. Bison foraging is an intense process, often with several bites taken with each step forward.

Bison are anatomically and physiologically adapted for the task of processing large amounts of relatively low quality forage. They have wide faces and mouths designed for ingesting large bites, often several plants at a time. (Compare the narrow, more delicate mouths of pronghorn and deer, "designed" for nibbling on individual plants.)

Mammals do not produce enzymes for digesting cellulose, a large component of relatively low-quality forage. But a ruminant digestion system allows symbiotic flora, mostly bacteria, to live within the digestive tract and digest forage, including some cellulose, benefiting the host bison. Bison have especially large rumens, the "digestion vats" that maintain ideal conditions for abundant bacteria. The large rumen and abundant bacteria are needed to process a bison's abundant forage intake. Larger ruminants, being less selective feeders, have larger rumens (relative to body size) than do smaller ruminants. I predict the rumen contents of a bison would amount to about 7-8% of the animal's body weight. In contrast, the rumen contents of a pronghorn are only about 4% of body weight.

Bacterial digestion is a relatively slow process. After a foraging bout, the rumen is full, and continued foraging is not possible. However, the ruminant will enhance the rate of forage digestion by regurgitating and rechewing forage. Cud chewing enhances digestion, facilitates depletion of the rumen contents, and allows initiation of a new foraging bout.

The rate of bacterial digestion of forage may be limited by a high ratio of carbon to nitrogen in the rumen substrate. This is common in low quality forages with high cellulose/protein ratios. Bison have adapted to this problem by efficiently reusing nitrogen. Much nitrogen from protein catabolism is recycled back into the rumen, rather than being excreted. Bison are more efficient at nitrogen recycling than are cattle, and they digest natural forage more completely than do cattle.[5]

In these and other ways, bison are preeminently adapted for foraging in grasslands. In prairies, grasses are abundantly and continuously distributed, allowing for efficient, abundant harvest. The large bison can not be as selective in foraging as are pronghorn and deer, or even elk. Yet, bison will optimize forage quality by habitat selection, more than by selecting plant species or plant parts. They will emphasize feeding in recently burned areas in a stage of "green-up";[6] and they may concentrate on swales and drainages where soil moisture enhances plant production, often replacing grasses with moisture-loving sedges. Sedges are a major component of some bison diets.

While grasses and sedges appear to be the favored forages in bison diets, the animals are capable of using forbs and shrubs, especially willow, in areas where the preferred grasses and sedges are less common. However, the diet of plains bison seldom contains more than 10 percent of woody plants. Bison are adapted as grazers, not as browsers.[7]

Disease Resistance and Accommodation

During long association with disease organisms, natural selection favors adaptations that reduce exposure and increase resistance of mammals to the negative effects of their pathogens. The disease host evolves. However, there is simultaneous evolution of the disease organism. The successful adaptive strategy of a parasite or pathogen includes methods for infecting and living within a host, reproducing, and being transmitted to yet another host before the first host dies. A disease organism that kills or debilitates its host before escaping to another host will be eliminated. This process of mutual evolution of host and disease is called "accommodation". (See Chapter 8 for more on disease accommodation.)

Gates et al. (2010) list nine diseases as threats to bison conservation. All are livestock diseases transmittable to and from bison. Perhaps all were unimportant to bison before domestic livestock, especially cattle, were widely distributed in North America. Further, it is likely that selective predation upon infected animals, especially by wolves, once maintained a reduced incidence of disease in bison. These diseases are therefore "novel" diseases in the evolutionary history of bison. At least three, anthrax, brucellosis and tuberculosis, were not present in North America before 1500, and are non-native, but "naturalized" diseases. Mutual evolution toward accommodation with these non-native diseases has been occurring for about 25 generations of bison.

A truly wild population will suffer losses to disease as natural selection favors and maintains disease resistance and accommodation. For wild bison, the novel and non-native character of some diseases predicts these losses may sometimes be large. In wildlife management, there is little recognition of this role of natural selection in disease resistance and accommodation. The prevailing paradigm is that wildlife populations should be "healthy" in the same way that domestic animals are healthy. However, wild bison must face their diseases head on. Natural selection should continue to provide evolution of disease resistance and accommodation with pathogens. Anything less will diminish wildness of bison. (In this sense, a sick animal is an appropriate component of a healthy, evolving ecosystem.)

Predator Defense and Evasion

Major components of the bison predator strategy are defense, escape and synchronized birthing. All involve behaviors common in "selfish herds". In a selfish herd, individual animals cooperate with and use other animals to enhance their own survival and reproduction, and perhaps the survival and reproduction of genetically related kin. In mutual defense, bison cooperate to the benefit of all animals in the herd. However, in group escape a bison is not only outrunning predators, but is seeking to outrun other bison. In evolution, altruism has its limits.

Defense. Mature bison are powerful, intimidating animals. Given its bulk, a bison is surprisingly agile. Bison have been observed to leap more than 6 feet to clear fences.[8] But the main weapons are a bison's head and horns. With powerful neck muscles, a bison can hook, lift and flip an opponent into the air. A biologist on the Wichita Mountains National Wildlife Refuge described a rutting bull that hooked and tossed another bull over its shoulder.[9] Sometimes, the horns will gore an enemy, causing potentially fatal wounds.

The defense strategy works best for bison in large herds. A lone bison cannot face and challenge several predators, such as a pack of wolves, at once. A lone cow is particularly unlikely to successfully defend her calf as wolves attempt to separate and kill it. In contrast, a herd of bison will cooperate to defend themselves and their calves. They will form a tight group, facing the enemy, with calves amongst or behind the adults.

Escape. During Pleistocene evolution of bison, the stand-and-defend strategy became less important with the extinction of some large predators, and less effective when human predators began using projectiles such as spears and arrows. A strategy of flight, outrunning and outlasting predators, evolved. Bison are physiologically and anatomically adapted for this behavior. With an extraordinary cardio-pulmonary system, a running bison can challenge all but the fastest horses, and outlast all of them by running for many hours over dry, hard prairie ground. This escape strategy requires precocial calves (Fig. 4.2). Newborn bison calves are on their feet within 10 minutes and able to run within 2 hours.[8]

Fig. 4.2. Newborn bison calves are precocial, standing within minutes and able to run within hours (Don MacCarter photo).

For a prime-age, healthy bison, the escape strategy has another, selfish, component. The escaping herd will expose the weakest individuals: the old, the injured and the sick. These individuals will lag behind the escaping herd. Wolves are alert to them, for they are easier and safer to attack and kill. In this manner, predation selects against the least fit bison and favors evolution and maintenance of strength, agility, endurance and disease-resistance in bison.

Part of the escape strategy is to leave predators behind. In a large, open prairie, bison may move many miles and may leave the home territory of a pack of wolves or a clan of humans that had found them.

The extreme of this escape strategy was the stampede, a phenomenon that may never be seen again. Early records of bison stampedes are remarkable.[10] Hundreds, even thousands of frenzied bison have charged pell-mell for miles across the plains with such speed and in such close proximity that any stumbling bison could be trampled. Observers heard the thundering roar of approaching bison hooves from miles away. It seems bison should have participated in such stampedes only if the risks of not participating exceeded those of stampeding. Indeed, when the threats were Pleistocene predators such as wolves, short-faced bears, American lions, or American cheetahs, the risks of not joining the stampede probably were large. However, very many bison were observed to die in such wild stampedes.

Synchronous Birthing is characteristic of many social ungulate species that have evolved with capable predators. With little flexibility in the gestation period, synchronous birthing depends upon having a synchronized breeding period. Synchronous birthing has a dual purpose in bison population dynamics. It is a predator evasion strategy and also a tactic to provide optimum use of a limited, predictable annual period of high quality forage, particularly for lactation.

Bison calves are vulnerable to predation by wolves and bears. They are most vulnerable during the first few weeks of life, and especially during the first few hours. However, newborn bison calves are precocial, as noted above.

Synchronous birthing is a gambling strategy. Predators using bison calves during the birthing season must spend some time eating and digesting their prey. They will spend additional time traveling to relocate a moving bison herd. Moreover, the number of predators within an area may be limited by territorial behavior. Thus, the number of calves that may be taken by predators during a short period is limited. If a large herd of bison cows gives birth during a short time, some of the new calves must evade predation. The larger the cow herd and the shorter the birthing period, the greater percentage of newborn calves that will survive. A bison cow that breeds during the peak of the rut, and calves during the peak of the calving period, provides her calf with a greater likelihood of escaping predation, especially if she lives within a large herd.

Calves born outside the peak birthing period will have a somewhat reduced chance of survival. In this way, predation reinforces birthing synchrony of the herd. There is selection against genes that allow departure from the peak birthing period.

In the USA south of Alaska, most bison no longer live with capable predators. However, bison in the Yellowstone area of the Rocky Mountains still live with bears and recently reintroduced wolves. In Yellowstone National Park, 80 percent of bison calves are born during 30 days, between April 25 and May 25.[11] Without effective predators in most bison herds, there will be reduced selection to maintain this birth synchrony, especially in environments where the annual flush of spring, high quality forage is less pronounced and less predictable.

Adaptations to the Social Environment

We can measure animal anatomy, and use chemistry and biophysics to measure animal physiology. However, animal behavior is a different kind of science. Bison adaptations to the social environment are largely a matter of behavior. Moreover, they largely involve bison communications. Bison use sight, sound, taste and smell to communicate.

We probably see better than do bison. However, when one bison looks at another, he knows just what he is looking for – and we do not. The elaborate hair pattern – beard, chaps, cape and head-bonnet – of a bison bull is a display pattern signaling virility and dominance to other bison.[12] With abundant patience, animal behaviorists have identified, we think, the meanings of some postures and movements of bison that are intended to communicate to other bison, often as threats or to communicate submission.

We know that the position of a bison's tail communicates the animal's mood. A tail held upwards, like a question mark, indicates a threat.

The environment of a large rutting group of bison is a pandemonium of grunts, groans, and roars. Bellowing bulls may be heard for miles. Clearly, there is vocal communication that we strain to understand. But is there more than we can hear? Do bison communicate with sound frequencies that are below our ability to detect?

We know bison communicate by "taste" as we see bulls testing the urine of cows for products of hormone catabolism that reveal estrus and willingness to breed (Fig. 4.3). Like many mammals, bull bison have vomernasal organs in the roofs of their mouths for this purpose. During the rut, bulls test cow urine frequently, sometimes nudging a reclining cow to stand and urinate. When the taste test indicates a cow is near ovulation, the bull will tend her and try to keep other bulls away (Fig. 4.4).

However, mammalian communication by scent is mostly beyond human capability to measure, if not to detect. No doubt, there is a large amount of mammal communication of which we are not aware. Somehow, probably by scent, cows communicate their physiologies to other females of the herd. This results in some synchrony of ovulations among the cows. In one herd, half the cows were bred within 4 days.[8]

Fig. 4.3. Bison bull testing cow for reproductive status. (Don MacCarter photo).

Fig. 4.4. Bison bulls tending cows during the Yellowstone rutting season.

Much bison social behavior, especially among bulls, is antagonistic. Ritualized postures and movements of the body, head and tail convey threats and submissiveness in establishing dominance/subordinance hierarchies. Especially during the rut, bellowing is an additional threat. Excessive wallowing can be a show of strength and energy (Fig. 4.5), augmented when a bull wallows in his own urine. What scents are communicated in this way? Within both sexes, larger and older animals are usually more dominant.

Fig. 4.5. Wallowing, an important social behavior of bison, influences the microhydrology and plant composition of bison habitat.

Outside the breeding season, antagonistic behaviors seldom result in significant physical conflict (Fig. 4.6). A subordinate bull will simply walk away from a usually larger bull. Conflicts waste time and consume energy, with risks of injury. It is better to continue foraging, ruminating, storing fat and growing. Fat will provide energy that may be needed during the rut when there is little time for foraging. Fat will be needed for the oncoming winter. Growth, for bulls, is the only way to future dominance and access to females.

Fig. 4.6. Bison bulls in a brief dominance dispute.

Even during the rut, subordinate bulls are usually displaced and moved by dominant bulls without physical contact. Dominance relationships have been established within bull-only groups during the non-breeding season. However, sometimes two bulls will decide to battle and the result may be awesome to observe. Two tons of bison, smashing heads, shoving and trying to hook one another, dust flying in all directions. In these contests, bulls are sometimes injured. Gored in the abdomen, a bull may die a lingering death due to infection.

The risks of challenging for dominance may be high; but the rewards can be great in terms of getting one's genes into future generations. For younger bulls, the risks of challenging an older, larger bull are especially great. So the strategy is to wait a year, after another summer of intense foraging and growth. The rewards are delayed. For older bulls, there are few, if any, years left. Future rewards are questionable; so the challenges are accepted and fearsome battles ensue.

A dominant bull will tend a cow in estrous. He will block her from entering the main body of the herd; and will threaten other bulls from coming near. However, the decision to breed is not his alone. As a cow nears her critical time, she may evade the tending, blocking bull and run through the herd, exciting other bulls. She will often approach a larger, more dominant bull and stand to be bred by him.[8]

This process of mate selection favors bulls that have successfully passed the tests of time and the environment. Genes of bigger, stronger, more alert, more agile, more energy efficient and disease resistant bulls are passed along. Mate selection has been a major factor determining and maintaining the characteristics of wild bison.

Wildness in Perspective

The above descriptions of bison adaptations are instructive, but inadequate. We have probed, tested, observed and analyzed bits and pieces from thousands of years of bison evolution. Results, published in cold science journals are impressive. But they are only a small window into the depth, diversity and complexity of what a wild bison is. To describe the whole animal, living and dying in a wild environment, we must resort to more broad but vague expressions, including wild, free, instinctive, even spiritual. Our studies of bison anatomy, behavior and physiology, of bison history and paleontology, add some definition and meaning to our more vague descriptions of the whole animal. And they demonstrate how much is unknown, and probably unknowable, of wild bison.

Wild bison are fellow travelers on this planet. Their genes retain ancient memories. Given the chance, they will still be bison – facing the blizzard head on, remembering and using a broad landscape, contesting for the right to breed, single-filing to water or to better forage, or thundering off to safety. It is the whole animal that we try to perceive and preserve for others to ponder. We can not preserve wild bison without wildness – and, for bison, wildness will be retained only in large wild places where natural selection operates.

Footnotes

[1] Anecdotal accounts of bison adaptations were reviewed by Dary (1974). In comparing ancient and modern bison, Guthrie (1990) provides a modern, academic approach to the study of bison adaptations to their environments. In truth, we have barely begun to investigate bison behavior and physiology.

[2] Lott (2002)

[3] Christopherson et al. (1978, 1979).

[4] Personal communication, Eric Cole, biologist, National Elk Refuge.

[5] Hawley et al. (1981).

[6] On the Wichita Mountains National Wildlife Refuge, Oklahoma, and elsewhere, bison selectively forage on recently prescribed-burned patches of habitat.

[7] Gates et al. (2010).

[8] Lott (2002).

[9] Personal communication, Walter Munsterman, biologist Wichita Mountains National Wildlife Refuge.

[10] See Gard (1959) for descriptions of bison stampedes.

[11] (Jones et al. (2009).

[12] Geist (1991).

Chapter 5

Wild Bison Populations

The previous chapter described wildness in bison by focusing primarily on the characteristics of individuals. Other attributes of wildness belong, not to individuals, but to populations of bison. Populations carry the genetic diversity of a species; they have sex-age structures and social structures. Populations fluctuate in abundance through time. Populations evolve, individuals do not. Here, I explore the roles of these population characteristics of wild bison and their implications for reestablishing a few wild plains bison herds.

"Wild" and "natural" are often used words, but they are seldom well defined. I tend to use the words synonymously. A truly wild population of native animals or a truly wild ecosystem is one that exists and functions with no impact from humans. In this sense, very few wildlife are completely wild. Impacts of our huge and dispersed human population are too pervasive. (Years ago, I wrote a college text on wildlife management. Now I realize that wildlife management is somewhat an oxymoron, as suggested long ago by Aldo Leopold who advised that the value of wildlife is inverse to the artificiality of the management system that produced it.[1])

One may argue that humans have been an important factor in the evolution of bison for many centuries. Native Americans, to some extent, managed bison numbers and distribution, and used fire to manage bison habitat. This argument is used to justify some degree of human intervention with wild bison herds as being natural and acceptable.

The argument can become esoteric and unproductive. Yet, it is important. Clearly, there are degrees of "wildness" based upon the degrees of human intervention with bison management. But what degrees and qualities of wildness should influence or dictate our goals for restoring wild plains bison?

We value wild plains bison for what they are – what they have become through their history of natural selection. In this history, intervention and selection by human activities have been significant, but not dominant. Therefore, if we are to retain wildness in plains bison, we must keep them in environments where the major forces of past evolution may continue, albeit in the context of an evolving North America. Relaxation or elimination of these selective forces will result in gradual changes in bison anatomy, physiology and behavior. Moreover, replacement of natural selective forces with human interventions can cause rapid changes in bison, leading to domestication as bison adapt to a captive or semi-captive environment.

Genetic Diversity

A wild, self-contained bison population should consist of at least 2000-3000 animals. Why is that? The answer lies primarily in the complicated field of population genetics.

Before Europeans arrived, bison were widespread in North America. There were millions of bison. Considering the historic records of bison mobility, and also the tendency for bison bulls to wander far, it is likely that interbreeding among most subpopulations was widespread. With few barriers and abundant gene exchange, there may have been few areas where bison were relatively isolated, allowing local adaptations to local conditions.

However, this view of an interbreeding megapopulation of bison is likely over-influenced by a historical record that emphasizes bison on the Great Plains. The degree of isolation among historical bison herds east of the Mississippi and west of the Rocky Mountains is unknown. A comparison of genetic characteristics of bison among eastern, central and western specimens of bison would be instructive in this regard. But there are few museum specimens of eastern and western bison. Geneticists have been "surprised" by the genetic diversity remaining in today's plains bison, considering the severe genetic bottleneck of very few animals that has occurred. But all of today's plains bison seem to have originated from the central herds. We do not know what genetic resources may have been lost forever with the passing of eastern and western plains bison.

We must begin discussion of bison genetics with definitions of several terms.

Genes and Alleles

Simply put, a gene is a portion of a chromosome that corresponds to some "unit" of inheritance.[2] Alleles are the various forms of a gene that exist within a population of animals. For each gene, an animal has obtained one allele from each of its parents. Alternative forms of alleles may cause different results in the offspring. Thus, for a gene that influences resistance to some disease, there may be alleles that favor resistance and alleles that do not.

Genetic diversity has two components: heterozygosity and allelic diversity.

Heterozygosity - and Inbreeding Depression

An animal having two different alleles for a specific gene is called heterozygous. An animal with two copies of the same allele is homozygous. For a population, the proportion of animals that are heterozygous for a particular gene is a measure of population heterozygosity. The proportion of animals that are homozygous is the population's level of homozygosity. Populations that are more genetically diverse have a greater proportion of heterozygous, rather than homozygous, genes.

Some alleles are dominant. Their effects upon inheritance are fully expressed no matter what form of the allele has been obtained from an animal's other parent. Other alleles are recessive, being expressed only when an animal has both forms of the recessive allele. To complicate matters, some alleles are co-dominant. In co-dominance, if a different allele is obtained from each parent, both are still expressed in determining traits of the offspring.

Deleterious alleles may negatively affect an animal's ability to survive or reproduce. Consequently, deleterious alleles have a reduced chance for passage to the next generation and tend to be removed from a population through natural selection. However, recessive deleterious alleles may persist within a population because, being recessive, they are not always expressed in an animal and therefore are not always exposed to natural selection. Even so, deleterious recessive alleles are generally not common in a population.

Closely related individuals, such as parents and offspring or siblings, tend to carry some of the same recessive deleterious alleles. Breeding between closely related individuals – inbreeding - increases the probability that some offspring will inherit the same deleterious recessive alleles from each parent. In this condition, homozygosity, the deleterious traits are expressed, debilitating the offspring. In addition, inbreeding reduces the probability that individuals will inherit the benefits from having multiple forms of beneficial codominant alleles. Thus, inbreeding tends to produce individuals that are inferior at survival and reproduction. Inbred mammals tend to exhibit low fecundity, reduced growth, poor juvenile survival and lowered resistance to diseases. These negative results of inbreeding are termed "inbreeding depression".

There are evolved behavioral mechanisms that minimize breeding between closely related mammals (outbreeding behavior). The relationship between population size and the effectiveness of these behavioral mechanisms has not been studied, to my knowledge. I expect these mechanisms to be less effective in smaller populations. Moreover, the behavioral mechanism to minimize inbreeding could be a genetically controlled trait that may be lost whenever natural selection is replaced or weakened by genetic drift or by artificial selection, as discussed below and in Chapter 8.

Small populations tend to accumulate closely related individuals, necessitating inbreeding. The probability of inbreeding depression in a population depends upon (1) the frequency of inbreeding among animals as determined by population size and by the effectiveness of outbreeding behavior and (2) the abundance of recessive deleterious alleles in the population (termed "genetic load").

Avoiding inbreeding depression may be accomplished by maintaining large populations. In domestication, inbreeding can be minimized by controlling breeding and replacing male breeders frequently. This avoids sibling, father-daughter and father-niece breeding. It is common practice in commercial bison herds and in many bison "conservation" herds. (Conservation herds are defined in Chapter 10.)

Genetic load of deleterious alleles seems to vary among species of mammals. Perhaps, due to normal social habits of some species, inbreeding has been more common during recent evolution, thus exposing and eliminating most recessive deleterious alleles. There is no evidence that plains bison have an unusually high or low genetic load compared to other mammals. However, the Texas State bison herd, originating from Charles Goodnight's captive bison and now kept at Caprock State Park, has experienced pronounced symptoms of inbreeding depression. This herd originated from but 13 animals in the 1880s, apparently was maintained at fewer than 250 for 110 years, and at about 40 animals during 1997-2002. It exhibited a low birth rate and low juvenile survival, probable in-uterine mortality, and sperm abnormalities. In recent years, the herd's growth rate has been essentially zero. To relieve this problem, bison from another herd have been bred into the Caprock herd. This managed outbreeding has reduced the symptoms of inbreeding depression.

For bison, about 400 - 500 animals may be required to avoid significant inbreeding.[3] This will vary with genetic load, with factors including the sex ratio and age structure of the population, and with the effectiveness of any behavioral outbreeding mechanisms. As noted above, inbreeding in smaller bison populations can be reduced by artificially controlling which bulls are allowed to breed. However, this replaces natural selection with human decisions and can lead to some degree of domestication.

Therefore, to avoid unacceptable levels of homozygosity and the risk of inbreeding depression, wild bison herds are most prudently maintained in populations of at least 400 animals. In Chapter 11, I note that 77% of the 44 herds of plains bison that are most important for conservation of the species in the USA fail to meet this standard.

However, the standard is usually academic, since a much larger population is required to avoid significant loss of allelic diversity in bison.

Allelic Diversity - and Evolutionary Potential

Allelic diversity is usually expressed as the average number of different alleles per gene-location (on a chromosome) in a population. A population with great allelic diversity has more evolutionary potential, compared to one with less allelic diversity. Thus, the ability of a population to evolve and adapt to a new or changing environment will be compromised by having a low allelic diversity. (Think of allelic diversity as the variety of colors on an artist's pallet. If the artist must select from few colors, the options for the resulting painting are limited.)

A population may have a limited allelic diversity because it originated with very few founders. There just weren't many different alleles to start with, and beneficial mutations that may add to allelic diversity are relatively rare events. Bison herds that originated from few founders are expected to benefit from an introduction of bison from herds with different genetic histories. This brings new alleles into the herd, enhancing its allelic diversity and its evolutionary potential.

For an established population, events that may increase the relative abundance of some alleles and reduce or eliminate other alleles can occur due to natural selection, to human intervention (artificial selection), or to random chance, usually referred to as genetic "drift".

Natural selection, with no or minimal influence by humans, is the benchmark of wildness. It is discussed later in this chapter. Artificial selection, or human intervention with the natural selection process, is discussed in Chapter 8.

Genetic drift is a change in the relative frequencies of alleles in a population due to random events that occur during reproduction and survival. Thus, chance determines which alleles are passed between generations, be they beneficial or harmful alleles.

A major source of genetic drift results from separation of

chromosomes with their alleles during the formation of ova and sperm. (Most cells have the "2N" number of chromosomes. When ova and sperm are formed in cell division, chromosomes are "split", leaving the reproductive cells with the "1N" number of chromosomes. Thus, uniting an ovum and sperm will form a new organism, again with the normal "2N" number of chromosomes.)

For the most part, random chance determines which of a pair of alleles are discarded into unused ova or sperm, and which alleles an offspring will obtain from each parent. In a large population, copies of most alleles are numerously replicated in many animals. Alleles that are discarded in some matings are retained in others, and allele frequencies in the second generation of a population will closely resemble allele frequencies in the first generation. Large changes in allele frequencies are unlikely because the vagaries of chance tend to "balance out" in large populations. Thus, an allele occurring in 25% of the animals in a large reproducing population is likely to occur in very nearly 25% of the next generation. However, if the reproducing population is small, a resulting allele frequency of 20% in the next generation is not improbable due to chance. (As an analogy, it is much more likely to get 3 heads in 4 coin flips than it is to flip 75% heads in 100 coin flips.) Moreover, in a third generation, the most probable allele frequency is no longer 25%. It is 20% (that of its parents) and it may, by chance, decline again.

In this manner, allele frequencies in a population will vary across generations. While new alleles are not added in this process, alleles may decrease in frequency and may disappear from a population when none of a certain allele happens to be transmitted across two generations. It matters not whether these alleles are beneficial or deleterious at enhancing survival or reproduction in the prevailing environment.

In addition to random events in forming ova and sperm, genetic drift may occur when random environmental events remove animals or otherwise prevent them from reproducing and passing their alleles to the next generation. Any bison may be struck and killed by lightning. Any bison may stumble and break a leg, reducing its ability to survive and reproduce. Several bison may break through ice and drown. These are essentially random events that may remove beneficial alleles from a bison herd.

Given enough time, genetic drift will eventually remove some alleles from a population, reducing its allelic diversity. However, the chances that alleles will be lost are greatest in small populations and for rare alleles. Scientists debate how large a population is necessary to assure retaining a desirable amount of allelic diversity. Variation in a population's sex ratio, age structure and breeding habits will influence the rate of losing alleles by genetic drift. Computer modeling suggests that a herd of 2000-3000 bison will lose an estimated 5% of its allelic diversity during each 100 years.[4] Smaller herds will lose even more of their allelic diversity. Note, we are already into the second century with plains bison existing only in pens and almost always with herds far smaller than this standard. This rate of loss will be significant for the future of plains bison. We do not know which alleles will be lost, nor understand their effects in determining traits of future generations of bison. The rarest alleles are most in jeopardy. Significantly, that part of the bison DNA that determines an animal's ability to detect and resist disease organisms is exceptionally diverse, but contains very many rare alleles that are most susceptible to loss.[5]

Moreover, genetic drift does not have to remove an allele from all animals in a population to weaken the effectiveness of natural selection. Alleles that enhance the animals' fitness have a random chance to be removed from many animals before their fitness benefits are realized and expressed in rates of survival and reproduction. Thus, "fit alleles" fare no better than do "unfit alleles". This weakening of natural selection will be most important in small populations.

Beyond allelic diversity, a bison population's ability to evolve and adapt to new and changing environments will be enhanced by the occurrence of beneficial mutations that add alleles to the herd. However, beneficial mutations are rare events. Their frequency of occurrence is directly related to the number of animals in a population. Thus a population of 2000-3000 bison is the minimum number of animals needed to preserve most evolutionary potential of bison for the foreseeable future. However, I hasten to note that some biologists recommend at least 5000 animals are needed to maintain genetic diversity and evolutionary potential for more than the foreseeable future.[6]

Based on our knowledge of the cattle genome, a bison carries about 22,000 genes. Most of these genes are common to all mammals and are not threatened to be lost across generations of bison. However, many thousands of genes are subject to natural selection, artificial selection, and genetic drift. Across a large bison population, some thousands of these genes are each represented by more than one form of the gene, that is, by different alleles in different animals. We know very, very little about which alleles are associated with what traits of bison, or about how alleles interact to determine bison characteristics.

A geneticist has suggested that our knowledge of bison genetics is akin to looking through one window of the Pentagon, and deducing what goes on inside. Moreover, I suggest that rather few of us have enough knowledge of genetics to find the Pentagon. With all this uncertainty, extreme prudence is justified in determining how we conserve bison for future generations.

Population Sex-age Structure

Sex Ratio. In a wild bison herd, there are about as many adult males as adult females. The sex ratio is near 1:1 because mortality rates are similar for bulls and cows. A result of half the population being bulls is that, outside the breeding season, there are numerous small groups of bulls scattered across the range (Fig. 5.1). These bulls are at least 3 years old and usually travel in groups of 1 to 5 animals. Some bulls wander long distances, a habit that exchanged genes among subpopulations and may have resulted in range expansions for bison in the past.

For most of the year, cows, calves, yearlings and young bulls aggregate into large herds, separate from adult bulls (Fig. 5.2). They generally use large patches of the best available forage. Implications of this sexual segregation for bison foraging efficiency, energy

Fig. 5.1. Older bison bulls typically travel alone or with only a few other bulls during most of the year.

Fig. 5.2. Except during the rut, most bison travel in large mixed groups of cows, calves, yearlings and a few young bulls.

conservation, predator risk and grazing impacts on vegetation are not entirely clear. Likely, separation of small bull-groups allows a more even distribution of grazing pressure across the bison range. Small patches of quality forage are used by small groups of bulls. These patches will not support the large, mixed-sex groups; at least not without negative effects of close competition among animals. Consequently, we should expect the larger, mixed-sex groups of bison to use the largest available patches of quality forage. Moreover, separation of bulls for much of the year results in less competition for forage with their own offspring. Natural selection should eliminate bulls that reduce the fitness of their own genes in the next generation.

Largest aggregations of bison occur during the rut, or breeding season (Fig. 5.3). An even adult sex ratio results in intense competition among bulls for access to breeding cows. Early in the rut, large, dominant bulls that have proven their abilities to survive and to efficiently use forage resources will obtain most of the breeding. This is a major component of natural selection. Bulls that have proven their fitness do most of the breeding. But, in large bison herds, these dominant bulls seem to tire of the energy-expensive rutting behavior. They may leave the rutting herd, and leave the breeding of those cows that achieve late-season breeding status to less-dominant bulls. Still, with an even sex ratio in a large bison herd, there are numerous less-dominant bulls and the natural selective values of competition among them persist. Moreover, cows are known to exert some selection for mates.[7]

In commercial bison herds, only a few bulls are needed to impregnate all the cows. Consequently, production from limited forage resources is maximized by "running" more cows than bulls. The natural selection values of bull competition, and of cows selecting mates, are reduced or lost. Moreover, the potential for inbreeding is increased. This intervention with natural selection is also practiced in many of the 44 conservation herds (Chapter 11) of plains bison because (1)

Rewilding Plains Bison

Fig. 5.3. Bison group sizes are normally largest during the rut, when old bulls join the mixed sex-age groups (R. Bailey photo).

many conservation herds are managed with incentives to produce and sell animals, just as in commercial herds; and (2) older bulls become more difficult to handle and therefore are more likely to be removed through culling at an earlier age compared to cows.

Age Structure. Age structure refers to the relative numbers of animals in each age class of a bison herd. Age classes might be year-cohorts, or – more generally – calves, yearlings, young adults, mature adults and aged animals.

Bison may live for 20 or more years. For bulls in wild herds, most breeding is accomplished by animals 8-12 years old. Cows usually produce their first calf at age 3 and may continue to produce beyond 15 years of age.

Survival and reproduction by older animals is an important component of natural selection. A bison's gene-based advantages for surviving, reproducing and leaving abundant genes in succeeding

84

generations will not be fully realized if the animal dies at an early age due to some random catastrophe or to artificial culling. In contrast, the advantages of the fittest bison will accumulate as the animal lives longer. Thus, having many old bison, at least 12-15 years of age, in a bison herd is an important contribution to natural selection. Artificially maintaining a young age structure reduces the effectiveness of this selection.

Age structures of wild bison herds will vary among herds and among years within herds. Bison herds living with wolves and bears usually have an older average age because calves and yearlings are more vulnerable to predation. Most increasing herds, perhaps rebounding from a few poor years of drought or severe winters, will have relatively more young animals. The sizes of calf crops and their early survival will vary among years, altering herd age structure.

On Antelope Island, Utah, a change in bison population age structure altered the herd's social structure. When the herd had been culled to maintain a younger age structure, the cow-juvenile bison normally dispersed into many small groups. After new culling practices established an older herd, the cow-juvenile bison aggregated into 2-3 large groups.[8] Implications of this change for natural selection have not been studied.

Since dominance is related to age and size of bison, the degree of competition faced by each individual can vary, not only with the number of competing animals, but with ages of competing animals. Thus, variation in herd age structure can contribute to variation of the intensity of natural selection for different survival and reproduction traits of bison. Fluctuating natural selection can be a mechanism for retaining genetic diversity in bison herds. This idea is developed more below, under "Population Fluctuations".

Competition, Dominance and Natural Selection

The social life of bison revolves around dominance and subordination. Most interactions either determine dominant and subordinate ranks, or are recognitions of already established ranks. Generally, larger and older bison are dominant over smaller and younger bison.[9] When resources are limiting, dominance enhances an animal's access to resources and therefore its fitness.

The major role of bull competition and dominance in determining reproductive success of bison bulls was discussed in Chapter 4. However, social rankings also partition access to resources among bison cows.[10]

Fig. 5.4. Note the pair of bison competing for one small patch of forage near the center of the photo.

Subordinate cows have been observed to clear snow from a patch of forage, only to be displaced from their feeding crater by a dominant cow. Even in summer, during foraging bouts, dominant cows spend more time foraging and less time moving and searching for forage, compared to subordinate cows. This suggests that dominant cows have claimed and defended patches of forage with the greatest forage density (Fig. 5.4). In environments with predators, dominance may provide a cow, and perhaps her calf, with access to the safest position in the interior of the herd. Such disparities, in winter or summer, enhance survival, growth and fat reserves of the dominant animal. This increases her ability to provide the most nutritious milk for her calf, and to attain sufficient weight to trigger ovulation and breeding in the next season. Likewise, the subordinate cow's ability to reproduce successfully is diminished. Dominance behavior therefore increases, not only the absolute number of the dominant animal's genes in subsequent generations, but – even more – the relative number in relation to genes of subordinate animals.

Population Fluctuations

In small bison herds, large fluctuations in numbers of bison should be avoided. Such fluctuations include periodic low numbers and will accelerate inbreeding and loss of genetic diversity. However natural fluctuations in population size have played an important role in determining selective forces that produced wild bison. When small herds are managed for stability of bison numbers, this component of natural selection is lost.

Stable wildlife populations are unusual. Most populations fluctuate without much notice. However, major declines and large increases are sometime obvious. Severe winters, periods of drought, periodic wildfires, and outbreaks of disease occur and fade away. Once, bison numbers responded to these vagaries of nature.

Healthy, wild bison populations fluctuate in abundance, and they live in environments where their habitat resources and their diseases and predators vary as well. However, it is not simply bison numbers; it is bison numbers in relation to the carrying capacity of their habitat that is uniquely important to the future of wild bison. Carrying capacity is the ability of the habitat to sustain a population. For large herbivores, forage quantity and quality are the most often considered elements of carrying capacity. Usually, they are the only elements considered. Carrying capacity will be determined by climatic factors such as moisture or drought that affect forage production, snow that determines forage availability, or by recent fire or recent grazing that affect available forage. Forage carrying capacity is constantly changing, within and among years.

The relationship of bison numbers to carrying capacity is termed "ecological density". A low ecological density is a few bison on abundant, quality habitat. A high ecological density is very many bison on limited or degraded habitat. In a wild bison ecosystem, bison numbers fluctuate, carrying capacity fluctuates, and ecological density varies accordingly. This natural variation is a characteristic of wildness.

I suggest that varying ecological density has been important in the evolution of wild bison. Factors of natural selection have varied in direction and degree between periods of low and high ecological density. High ecological density, often called "crunch time", generates selection for high levels of foraging efficiency, energy maintenance, and willingness to compete for forage. Aggressive bison adapted behaviorally and anatomically to cold, with stout digestive systems and energy-efficient physiologies have resulted. These characteristics are in jeopardy in most conservation herds of bison because bison numbers are maintained at artificially stable and low ecological densities. Crunch time never comes, and selection for these traits of wild bison is relaxed.

These selective factors operating at high ecological densities of bison seem obvious. But, are recurring periods of low ecological density equally important for maintaining some traits of wild bison? The answer is more speculative.

Bison bulls with a genetic tendency to divert a greater proportion of their nutritional resources toward growth of display anatomy – large horns, long beards and luxurious leg chaps – may be disadvantaged in periods of high ecological density, when a more conservative strategy is more successful, especially for survival. But they may be more successful than bison with more conservative nutritional/growth strategies during periods of low ecological density when forage is abundant and available. (Admittedly, there is much epigenetic variation in bison growth as animals respond to nutritional conditions. However, this does not preclude some gene-based variation in growth patterns that may be exposed to natural selection.)

Implications of varying ecological density for natural selection of reproductive strategies of bison bulls are not clear. Bulls will compete aggressively for mates at either high or low ecological density. Energy-expensive competition for mates may be more intense at low ecological density when expenses can easily be recovered in the abundant foraging habitat. At high ecological density, dominant bulls may die earlier or may retire from the rutting groups relatively early, leaving some cows to be bred by less-dominant, perhaps younger bulls.

At high ecological densities, most cows do not breed until they are 2 or even 3 years old. Many do not breed every year because their physiology requires them to put on sufficient fat reserves before achieving breeding status. For each cow bison, the emphasis is to assure personal survival while producing a few, high quality calves with high probabilities for their own survival in a habitat with a high ecological density of competing bison.

In contrast, during periods of low ecological density, cows with less conservative reproduction strategies may be favored. The costs of producing a calf at an early age, or in successive years, can easily be made up in the abundant habitat. With abundant forage and few competitors, that is, low ecological density, cows with a "gambling" reproduction strategy can be successful. They gamble that breeding early before completing their own growth, or that breeding every year with perhaps less sufficient fat reserves, can still be successful. During periods of low ecological density, the gambling strategy may provide more calves and genes in the next generation than will the conservative reproduction strategy.

Thus, a fluctuating ecological density should provide alternating variation of natural selection that maintains the genetic bases for both conservative/competitive and gambling/less aggressive animals in the herd.

However, the common practice of managing bison herds at constant population sizes, usually at low ecological density, should diminish genetic diversity. The gene pool becomes specialized for living at one constant ecological density. This is a form of "stabilizing selection". Fluctuating ecological density is a much neglected aspect of wildness in plains bison conservation.

In addition to the genetic aspects of varying ecological densities of bison, I would expect the ecological functions of bison – their impacts upon plants and other animals - will vary with bison numbers and bison ecological densities. Some functions will be intensified, or reduced or lost when bison are artificially maintained at a constant number of animals. There has been little study of the implications of fluctuating bison numbers for all the other species that share grasslands with bison.

Natural Selection and Evolution

Evolution is any change across generations in the types and relative frequencies of alleles. New, beneficial and successful alleles are a rare occurrence and they contribute very slowly to evolution. However, alteration of the selective forces, including genetic drift, working on the existing array of genes in a population, may cause more rapid – though not always obvious – evolutionary changes. These changes are permanent when alleles are lost.

Bison evolution has not ended. Genetic change is most rapid in small herds subjected to a preponderance of artificial selection based on human decisions – leading to domestication. This is most obvious in commercial bison herds. But genetic change is occurring in our "conservation herds" as well. In a few studies of bison genetics, detectable changes in herd genomes have occurred in as few as 5 to 8 generations (40 to 64 years).[11] One study suggests that disease management interventions have already altered the genetic compositions of some bison herds with respect to their natural resistance to brucellosis.[12]

If we are to retain wild bison for future generations, we must address the process of evolution and the combined effects of few founders, cattle-gene introgression, inbreeding, genetic drift and artificial selection in weakening or replacing natural selection. As we pass the bison genome to succeeding generations, we give too little thought to what this legacy will be.

Footnotes:

[1] Leopold (1933) referred to the recreational value of wildlife being compromised by artificial management, but all other wildness values (Chapter 6) are also diminished.

[2] Geneticists, bear with me. I am trying to communicate a necessary amount of genetics to the layperson. Most are familiar with "genes" and "chromosomes". "Alleles" and "loci" are unfamiliar terms, and I have avoided the latter.

[3] Gross et al. (2006) suggested 400 bison as needed to retain 90% heterozygosity over 200 years. Perez-Figueroa et al. (2010) concluded 500 bison would retain 95% heterozygosity over this period. What level of loss of heterozygosity is "significant" is a judgement call. However, we should have high standards for at least a few bison herds somewhere in the USA.

[4] Perez-Figueroa et al. (2010). The computer modeling of gene flow across generations conservatively assumes no effective outbreeding behavior in a Yellowstone bison population of this size. While some outbreeding behavior may, and probably does, exist, its role in these population genetics is unknown. In managing the only large, almost-wild population of bison south of Canada, prudence suggests accepting the implications of this study.

[5] This important region of mammal DNA related to disease resistance is termed the "major histocompatibility complex". I used the extensive review provided by Wikipedia.org for information.

[6] Traill et al. (2009). About 5000 is the estimated number of animals needed for alleles lost to genetic drift to be matched by the same

number of alleles gained through mutations. Thus, decline of allelic diversity would be 0.

[7] Lott (2002).

[8] Personal communication, Steve Bates, biologist, Utah Department of Natural Resources.

[9] Roden, C., H. Vervaecke and L. Van Elsacker. (2005).

[10] Lott (2002).

[11] Halbert et al. (2012).

[12] Seabury et al. (2005).

Chapter 6

Values of Wild Plains Bison

The several values of all wildlife are largely taken for granted by most Americans. Most of us enjoy seeing wildlife and we support wildlife conservation. Perhaps it is a part of human nature to wonder at all the diverse, colorful, interesting critters that we find near home and especially in places we refer to as "wild". Just seeing a mountain lion, grizzly bear, gray wolf – or wild bison – is a unique and memorable event for most Americans. For many, it is a once in a lifetime.

But economists and others who must track costs, benefits and values in public management plans and environmental impact statements find the pervasive "Oh wow!" attitude of Americans toward wildlife to be a bit "fuzzy" for analytical purposes. So it behooves us to analyze, "What good are wild animals?" Too often, a poor and incomplete answer to this question has diminished the future of wildlife in competition with other, often commercial, resources that compete for space on the American landscape.

I will briefly describe the types of values inherent in all wildlife, with emphasis on wild bison.

Recreational Value

Recreational value of wildlife is very personal and recognized by nearly everyone. It is the joy, wonder, excitement, fascination and accomplishment inherent in observing, feeding, hunting, fishing and studying wildlife. For family members and friends, it includes the camaraderie of experiencing the natural world together.

The above definition of recreational value of wildlife relies on human emotions in response to wildlife. Those who would push wildlife aside for usually commercial purposes often criticize this value of wildlife as too emotional – still to "fuzzy" for hard core analysis. However human life is an emotional experience. Do we discount the value of human life because it is "too emotional"?

For each of us, the recreational value of wildlife increases in proportion to our understanding of the wildlife we observe and pursue. The beauty of a slant of pintails approaching a marsh, beauty that meets the eye, is enhanced by beauty that meets the educated mind when one knows from whence the pintails have come and to where they must go for winter quarters. There is very much "Oh wow!" in the life histories of wildlife.

While recreational values of wildlife are described in emotional terms, they can be measured in hard dollars. The question is, "What are Americans willing to pay to sustain and access these recreational values of wildlife?" The question cannot be answered precisely because wildlife is a publicly-owned resource. Much of the cost of access to wildlife (hunting licenses, park entry fees) is limited by public policy. Otherwise, the poorest Americans would be priced out of the market. In this sense, the full recreational value of wildlife is not tested as it would be if a private entrepreneur owned our wildlife and priced access to it in order to maximize profits. Still, the amount of money that Americans do spend to access and enjoy wildlife is large, and is a minimum estimate of their willingness to pay for wildlife – that is, of how highly they value their wildlife.

In 2006, 87.5 million Americans spent over $137 billion on hunting, fishing and wildlife viewing in the United States.[1] More pertinent to this book, during 2010 3.64 million visitors spent over $334 million visiting Yellowstone National Park where the major attractions are Old Faithful geyser, wolves and bison.[2] The recreational value of wildlife is not trivial (Fig. 6.1).

Commercial Value

Commercial values of wildlife are measured in cold, hard dollars. While dollars spent by the recreating public may measure the recreational value of wildlife, those same dollars are income to those who provide equipment, goods and services to the recreationists, or sell access to wildlife on private lands. In rural areas, hotels, campgrounds, restaurants, gas stations and sporting goods stores depend upon local wildlife to bring in their customers (Fig. 6.2).

Guiding and outfitting businesses are totally dependent upon available wildlife. Gateway communities to national parks and wildlife

Fig. 6.1. Tourists line up to observe the bison herd, Theodore Roosevelt National Park (R. Bailey photo).

Fig. 6.2. Bison attract tourists and support local economies.

refuges are especially aware of this commercial value. It is estimated that people visiting Yellowstone National Park to see the sights, including bison, create nearly 4,900 local jobs.[2]

In addition, the value of meat and other products obtained when public wildlife are reduced to private possession through regulated hunting or fishing has commercial value. Bison are our largest big game species. A 1000-pound bison carcass will yield over 300 pounds of quality, low-fat meat.

The commercial value of bison is unique, however. I am not aware of any state that does not permit private ownership of bison as domestic livestock. Of the 44 "conservation" herds of plains bison on native range, 10 are privately owned, including 9 owned by the Nature Conservancy. Excess bison from these herds are sold on the open market. Income from bison sales is used to cover expenses of owning and managing the land and bison. Many public bison herds are managed similarly. The usually annual roundups and sale of public bison provide income for managing several public bison herds and public parks, including Custer State Park, South Dakota and Antelope Island, Utah. Three of the 4 largest plains bison herds on native range depend upon annual sales of bison to finance bison management.

Scientific Value

Wildlife have unique value as objects of research. It is precisely because we do not fully understand the anatomy, physiology and behavior of wild animals, nor the workings of wild populations and wild ecosystems, that we should restore and save some wild areas for scientific study.

The most prominent example of scientific value has been Charles Darwin's study of wildlife around the world and especially in the Galapagos Islands, resulting in the most basic principle of all biology – evolution. But we continue to learn from wildlife in such fields as population dynamics, behavior, navigation and pathology. Results have implications for how we manage the world and ourselves.

Our cattle industry manages bovine diseases with vaccinations, deworming, antibiotics and selective slaughter of infected animals. In contrast, wild bison would evolve with their disease organisms, and would develop some disease resistance. Given the recent advances in gene therapy, it is not unreasonable to predict that one day genes for disease resistance could be transferred from wild bison to domestic cattle.[3]

Humans are committed to monotonizing the world into an artificial, domestic environment dictated by, usually short-term, human needs. Wildlife and wild environments can serve as valuable counterpoints of comparison, so we may know what we have done to the world, and may better understand our options.

Ecological Value

Wildlife are valuable as integral parts of complex ecosystems. The numerous interactions among plants, animals, soils and water serve to create and maintain these ecosystems of many interdependent parts. If an ecosystem, such as Yellowstone National Park, has value, then all of its components contribute to that value. Removing or diminishing one species from such an ecosystem may cause perturbations throughout much of the system, diminishing its total value.

In this respect, bison were a "keystone species" on the Great Plains of North America.[4] Their interactions with prairie ecosystems were listed in Chapter 3 and are important enough to repeat here. Bison influenced the habitats and behaviors of many native species. Their periodic intensive grazing and wallowing maintained species and structural diversity in the vegetation. Bison wallows may seem too small to have been a significant component of the ecology of the Great Plains. However, there may have been 100 million wallows affecting vegetation and distribution of soil moisture. Bison provided disturbed habitat needed by plants that are unwelcome "weeds" in today's production-oriented livestock management. Disturbed sites supported animals, such as mountain plovers, and prairie dogs with numerous plants and animals that use prairie-dog towns.

Bison supported wolves that no longer exist on the vast majority of native bison range. Their carcasses fed a host of scavenger species including coyotes, bears, eagles, ravens, and even small birds that picked maggots and suet from bison remains. A dead bison is part of a living grassland ecosystem. In the end, the carcass site provides nutrient-rich soil supporting quality forage plants that are especially adapted to such sites.

The effects of bison cascaded through prairie ecosystems. Each spring, shed bison hair was used as insulating nest material by numerous grassland birds. Buffalo birds (now we call them cowbirds) evolved to feed on the backs of, and under the feet of, abundant bison. This commitment to feeding on and with bison, and the bison's great mobility, would not allow buffalo birds enough time for nesting in any one place. Consequently, buffalo birds adapted as nest parasites, laying their eggs in the nests of other birds, then moving on to follow bison. Thus, there are implications of bison for buffalo birds, for other prairie birds, and for the insect and plant foods of other birds, as well as for their predators.

Ecological values of bison are now diminished and rare. Cattle, especially with production oriented grazing, do not provide all these ecological values.[5] Cattle ranching tends to monotonize the range, converting as much land as possible into one condition that maximizes meat production. Moreover, a majority of the bison conservation herds are managed in ways that limit the ecological values of plains bison. A recent treatise on the future of plains bison declared, "The plains bison is for all practical purposes ecologically extinct within its original range."[6]

Esthetic, Historical, Cultural and Religious Values

These values of wildlife are diverse and personal. Esthetic value includes the roles of wild animals in art, literature and music (Fig. 6.3). The affection of contemporary Americans for wildlife is illustrated by the fact that wild animals are among the most frequently depicted icons in the recently minted series of state 25-cent pieces. Moreover, bison are the most frequently depicted species of wildlife – on the quarters of Kansas, North Dakota and Montana. (Admittedly, Montana depicts only a bison skull. Perhaps this is appropriate. As I write, Montana has no public herd of wild bison. However, the irony is that state laws in Kansas and in North Dakota do not recognize bison as a wildlife species.)

Fig. 6.3. Bison in art: depicting pair on the windy Great Plains. TNC statue, Tallgrass Prairie Preserve, Oklahoma.

Study of history is a necessary component for understanding the human condition. If we do not know our history, we can not know who we are. Particularly in the American West, wildlife have played important roles in American history. Bison and beaver have been prominent. If there is value in the joy and intellectual pursuit of reading history, there must be value in seeing and experiencing some of the wild environments in which our history occurred. What will we answer when our grandchildren ask, "Where are the bison as seen by Coronado, Sitting Bull, Lewis and Clark and John Colter?"

Reverence and respect for nature are prominent in some religious beliefs. Bison were, and remain, an essential component in the religions of Native Americans of the Great Plains. While most Americans ascribe to religions that preach dominion over the earth and all its creatures, the tyranny of the majority should not belittle the personal beliefs of others. Further, there are religious arguments for restoring and maintaining at least some examples of the creation, unfettered by intense human intervention.

We humans are constrained to live in one time, and for most of us, in one or a few places. But, with knowledge of other times and other places, we may expand our mental horizons. Having some wild bison to observe, study, and wonder at should always contribute to that expanded mental horizon for the people of North America.

The Value of Wildness in Bison

As noted in Chapter 8, wildness is not an absolute. It may be diminished along a continuum from wild to semi-wild to semi-domestic to domestic. The case for wildness values of bison is a discussion of how the above values are affected, reduced and lost along the wildness – domestication continuum.

Wildness is the most unique and irreplaceable characteristic of wildlife. Moreover, in our increasingly populated, developed and human-controlled world, wildness is everywhere diminished and more rare than it once was. Increasing rarity of a resource is expected to generate increasing value, according to concepts of supply and demand. However, if the public is unaware of the characteristics and requirements of wildness, the decline and disappearance of wildness may go unnoticed. This has occurred with plains bison in the United States.

Values of Wild Plains Bison

Increasing wildness of animals and greater public appreciation of the meaning of wildness will enhance most or all the above wildlife values. The hunting community has recognized this by instituting a concept of "fair chase" as a hunting ethic. Taking of animals, raised and perhaps artificially fed within a fenced area, perhaps harvested over bait, is looked upon with disdain. (Yet the commercial practice persists among some who have little appreciation for wildness.)

Not long ago, black bears begged for candy bars and sandwiches along the roads of Yellowstone National Park. The Park Service maintained tiers of seats for visitors to watch grizzly bears competing for food at a garbage dump. It seems tourists from Chicago might have saved travel costs and experienced just as much by viewing bears, sans garbage, at the Lincoln Park Zoo. Thankfully, these practices have ended in Yellowstone. Today, glimpses of bears in Yellowstone are less common, and more valued.

Compare the esthetic value of viewing Yellowstone bison as they interact with wolves in a snowy landscape to the half-loaf of seeing an ear-tagged herd of bison, with few bulls and no old animals, across the fence of some limited, managed preserve. Has the viewer seen wild bison, or visited an outdoor zoo?

And yet, commercial values of semi-wild or semi-domestic bison can be large. There is a market for bison trophies from herds that are being domesticated. The market for bison meat from managed herds is expanding. In 2010, 14 thousand tourists brought their dollars to Custer State Park, South Dakota, to view the annual bison roundup (Fig. 6.4). Bison were herded by western-dressed riders, some with chaps and handle-bar mustaches, flying the American and South Dakota flags on horseback, and backed up by four-wheel drive pickups (Fig. 6.5). Did these tourists consider whether they had seen wild bison, or a circus?

The scientific value of wild bison can not be compromised. We may not study predator-prey relationships in a limited bison range where predators are not welcome for reasons including that they would decrease the productivity of the bison herd. We may not study the

Fig. 6.4. A few among several thousand who spent their recreation dollars observing the Custer State Park bison roundup in 2010.

Fig. 6.5. The "bison circus" at Custer State Park, SD.

natural mechanisms of disease resistance and accommodation in vaccinated bison herds. We may not study the social relations of wild bison by viewing a herd with a skewed sex- and age structure. Most importantly, the scientific value of a wild bison range as a control area for comparison against the rest of the managed world will be reduced as any component of wildness is diminished.

The future of wild plains bison and their values in the United States will depend upon the political will of our people, relying upon public understanding of the characteristics and requirements of wildness in bison. If intensively managed bison on small reserves will satisfy most Americans, because they do not understand and appreciate wildness, then wild plains bison have no future in the United States.

Can Americans get along without restoring and maintaining examples of wild bison? Of course they can. But for many Americans, something is missing. The bottom line is that wild plains bison on a few large reserves of wild grassland would add diversity to our landscape and to our lives. We pride ourselves in maintaining a free country. Real freedom demands, not only a lack of restrictions, but an abundance and diversity of opportunities – opportunities to live, to err, to learn, to achieve, to experience a great portion of what life on our diverse planet has to offer. In a world where humans increasingly restrict their own freedom by crowding and monotonizing their environment, wild bison should be retained, at least as a symbol of what we have sacrificed in domesticating and civilizing ourselves.

Footnotes

[1] These are data generated by the U.S. Fish and Wildlife Service, reported by Southwick Associates in "The economics associated with outdoor recreation, natural resources conservation and historic preservation in the United States" for The National Fish and Wildlife Association.

[2] from Yellowstone National Park news release, February 28, 2012.

[3] In a very technical paper, Seabury et al. (2005) provide evidence of gene-based resistance to *Brucella* infection in bison.

[4] Gates et al. (2010), Knapp et al. (1999).

[5] Fuhlendorf et al. (2010).

[6] Freese et al. (2007).

Chapter 7

Major Ecotypes of Wild Plains Bison

A wildlife ecotype is a population or set of populations that live in and interact with a unique environment. Plains bison living in the tallgrass prairie of the southeastern plains are a distinctly different ecotype from plains bison living in a shrub-steppe at high elevation in a Colorado inter-mountain valley. These bison will exhibit different behaviors. Food habits must vary with the types, abundance and distribution of the vegetation. Patterns of forage availability will influence normal group sizes and competition within bison herds. Differences in forage quality and seasonal availability, and differences in winter severity, may influence birth and death rates and population dynamics. Differing seasonal phenologies will determine optimum times of the year for birthing and lactation.

Moreover, the ecological impacts of bison will vary among environments. The roles of bison interacting with vegetation, soils, hydrology and fire regimes will differ across climatic and vegetation zones.

Ecotypes need not be genetically different. Rather, ecotypes illustrate the plasticity of responses within the single genome. Without restoring multiple ecotypes of bison, we will be less able to observe and understand the full adaptive syndrome of plains bison, and bison will not be able to fulfill their necessary roles in restoring examples of some native ecosystems. In this regard, IUCN has stated, "to maintain biodiversity and evolutionary potential, it is important to not dismiss any form of differentiation within a species."[1]

However, there are bound to be different natural selective forces in markedly different environments. Existence of bison in a variety of environments will be necessary to enhance and maintain genetic diversity of the overall bison genome.

Biogeographers have identified 17 vegetation/habitat types within native plains bison range of the United States. A group of bison biologists suggests that ideal restoration of plains bison would include herds in each of these 17 areas, noting that it may take 100 years to accomplish.[2] For 5 of these habitat types, over 90% of the land is already well-developed for agricultural and urban purposes. For most of these types, the land is divided into complex mosaics of mixed-public and mostly private holdings. These facts create major opposition to, and difficulties for, wild bison restoration. Restoration of meaningful numbers of wild bison across a large area in each of the 17 major vegetation types seems to be a foregone opportunity. At least, there is no assurance that it can or will happen. Even if it will happen, the process must begin in only one or a few habitat types, and it must begin soon if we are to restore wildness of plains bison.

I therefore suggest that Americans begin the process of restoring plains bison by concentrating on five major ecotypes of bison. This is a realistic short-term goal and a place to start now. I suggest we concentrate on restoring plains bison in the northern Great Plains, central Great Plains, southern Great Plains, western Mountains, and in the Great Basin/Columbia Basin. It is a goal shaped as much by on-the-ground realities of land use and ownership as by bison biology and ecology. For practical purposes, I delineate these ecotypes with state boundaries, despite the biological reality that bison ecology will vary largely across boundaries of major vegetation types as they respond to patterns of soils and climate. However, the political realities of state laws and politics will predominate to determine bison restoration, not the complex ecological patterns on the ground. I suggest the reader pay particular attention to the plains bison ecotype whose range includes the reader's home state.

My discussions below include descriptions of some of the habitat diversity existing within each of the 5 ecoregions. For each region, a reserve for bison restoration must be both large and ecologically diverse to provide bison with choices for selecting habitat and forage in all seasons. Such choices are mechanisms of natural selection that will be necessary to maintain efficient habitat use and acute senses of wild bison. A diverse environment will maintain genetic diversity of bison. A monotonous environment will not.

Major Ecotypes of Wild Plains Bison

Northern Great Plains Bison

In the northern Great Plains, wild bison may be restored somewhere in the Dakotas, northeast Wyoming or eastern Montana. However, bison are not legally recognized as state wildlife in northeast Wyoming or North Dakota. In South Dakota, only penned herds of bison in parks are recognized as wildlife.

This area challenges bison with warm to occasionally hot summers and long, cold winters. Temperatures may vary between recorded extremes of minus 60 and 120 degrees F. Wind blows much of the time, occasionally generating blizzard conditions, but locally expressed as warming, "snow-eating" Chinook winds along the east slopes of the Rocky Mountains. Most of the country is semi-arid, receiving an average of 10 to 17 inches of precipitation per year. But prolonged droughts are common. The driest areas are concentrated westward in the rain shadow of the Rocky Mountains.

There is much topographic diversity in the northern plains. To the east are flat and gentling rolling plains. The prairie pothole region in the northeast, a legacy of Wisconsin glaciation, once provided an abundance of productive herbaceous wetlands that no doubt were used by plains bison. About half these wetlands have been permanently drained and others are more ephemeral than they once were. In the more arid west, are badlands, buttes and several island mountains, including the extensive Black Hills. Other island mountains include the Turtle, Bear Paw, Castle, Crazy, Highwood, Judith, Little Belt, Snowy, Bull, and Pryor Mountains, plus the Sweet Grass Hills and the Long Pines area. Many rivers and thousands of miles of smaller, sometimes intermittent, streams traverse the northern Plains. The largest rivers are associated with extensive "breaks" of rough and sometimes steep country.

The major vegetative pattern of the Northern Great Plains is an east-to-west progression from the more moist tallgrass prairie of far eastern Dokatas to the arid shortgrass plains of eastern Montana. Between these extremes, covering most of the Dokatas, is a sea of grass, a vast transition area of mixed-grass prairie.

Rewilding Plains Bison

Principle grasses of the tallgrass region include big- and little bluestem, switch grass and Indian grass. However, this region of fertile soils and adequate moisture is almost all plowed cropland today. To the west, the dry shortgrass prairie supports blue grama, buffalo grass, western wheatgrass and other arid-adapted species. There is considerable shrub-steppe, usually with sagebrush. The transitional mixed-grass zone contains elements of short- and tallgrass prairies, depending upon local topography, aspect and soils – major factors determining soil moisture. Thus, there are blue grama and buffalo grass on the driest sites, with western wheatgrass, needlegrass and Indian ricegrass on more moist sites and in wetlands, along rivers and streams and on north aspects.

This major east-west pattern associated with moisture is interrupted by floodplain forests, largely of cottonwood, along major rivers; by pine-juniper woodlands on island mountains and foothills; and by largely barren badlands that mostly support plant species of the shortgrass zone.

The great climatic, topographic and vegetative diversity of the northern Great Plains once provided mobile bison with many seasonal options for finding available, nutritious forage during all seasons and weather conditions.

Restoring wild bison on a large public reserve in the northern Great Plains would benefit very many grassland species that are now threatened, endangered, declining or rare. Some of the more notable species, including elk which are uncommon in North and South Dakota, are listed in Chart 7.1. Periodic severe winters with deep snow have been devastating to pronghorn herds on the northern plains. No doubt, pronghorn once benefited during these tough times by using bison trails in the snow and feeding on tidbits left in bison feeding craters.

Rural, agriculture-based human populations have been declining in the western, drier half of the northern Great Plains for many decades (Figs. 7.1, 7.2) For example, populations in several counties of eastern Montana declined by 10 to over 20 percent during 2000-

2009. Billings County, North Dakota where the headquarters of Theodore Roosevelt National Park is located has but 783 residents and its population declined 12% during 2000-2010. Decades ago, Deborah and Frank Popper correctly predicted declining human populations and economic conditions on the Great Plains.[3]

Fig. 7.1. Across the western Great Plains, relics persist from an agrarian human population that has been declining for almost 100 years.

Eight largest conservation herds of plains bison in the northern Great Plains are: Custer State Park, SD (1100 bison), Badlands National Park, SD (600), Wind Cave NP, SD (400), Theodore Roosevelt NP South, ND (350), Theodore Roosevelt NP North, ND (175), Ordway Prairie, TNC, SD (300), American Prairie Reserve, MT (200 and growing) and Cross Ranch, TNC, ND (200). (TNC = The Nature Conservancy.) Each of these herds currently has several limitations for maintaining wild plains bison, including small populations, limited size and diversity of range, legal and political constraints, and other issues, discussed in Chapter 11.

Three large areas of mostly contiguous public land provide very good opportunities for restoring wild bison on the northern Great Plains - in Montana, in North Dakota and in South Dakota.

Chart 7.1. Prominent rare or declinging species of concern in the Northern, Central and Southern Great Plains that could benefit from establishing a large prairie reserve with plains bison.

	Northern Plains	Central Plains	Southern Plains
FISHES			
Arkansas darter		KS, CO	
Flathead chub		KS, CO	
Arkansas River speckled chub		KS	
Pearl dace	MT, ND, SD	NE	
Topeka shiner FE		NE, KS	
Arkansas River shiner FT		KS	NM, OK
AMPHIBIANS			
Great Plains narrowmouth toad		CO, NE	
REPTILES			
Milksnake		CO, NE	
Hognose snake	MT, ND, SD	KS	
Smooth greensnake	MT, ND	NE	TX
BIRDS			
Ferruginous hawk	ND	CO, KS, NE	TX
Greater prairie-chicken	ND	KS, NE	
Lesser prairie-chicken FC		CO, KS	TX
Sage grouse FC	MT, ND	CO	
Long-billed curlew	MT, ND	CO, KS, NE	

110

Chart 7.1 continued

Mountain plover	MT	CO, KS, NE	TX
Piping plover FT	MT, ND, SD	CO, KS, NE	NM, OK, TX
Eskimo curlew FE	SD	KS, NE	
Short-eared owl	ND	KS, NE	
Burrowing owl	MT, ND	CO, KS, NE	TX
Sprague's pipit FC	ND	KS	
Sedge wren	MT, ND	NE	
Sharp-tailed sparrow	MT, ND		NM
Baird's sparrow	ND	KS	
Chestnut-collared longspur	ND	KS	
MAMMALS			
Black-tailed prairie dog	MT, ND	CO, KS	TX
Swift fox	ND, SD	CO, NE	
Black-footed ferret FE	MT, ND, SD	CO, KS, NE	TX
Plains elk	Uncommon	Rare	

FE = federal endangered species; FT = federal threatened species; FC = federal candidate.
Listed states also have some category of special rare status.

Rewilding Plains Bison

The best and largest area of diverse, mostly contiguous public land is centered on the Charles M. Russell National Wildlife Refuge and the Upper Missouri River Breaks National Monument in northeast Montana. The Refuge and Monument are surrounded by much additional federal land managed by the Bureau of Land Management, and small areas of state land. In all, there are several hundred square miles of mostly contiguous public land. Part of this landscape is depicted in Map 7.1.[4] In addition, the nearby Fort Belknap Indian Reservation could become a cooperator in restoring wild bison. Much of this diverse area has relatively little intermingled private land, and some landowners are bison friendly, including the American Prairie Reserve. Ideally, strategic areas of intermingled private land could be acquired over time as they become available from willing sellers. However, most of the public land is now leased for private livestock grazing; whereas there are no native wild bison, not on the federal "multiple use" lands, nor on the Wildlife Refuge. This area presents the best opportunity for restoring a large free-ranging herd of wild plains bison in the contiguous United States. A recent poll by the National Wildlife Federation indicated that about 70% of Montana voters favored restoring wild bison on the Charles M. Russell National Wildlife Refuge. The social and ecological history of this area has been described in Manning's "Rewilding the West".[5]

The Little Missouri National Grasslands in North Dakota offer a second opportunity for bison restoration on the northern Great Plains. Two units of Theodore Roosevelt National Park, with fenced bison, are imbedded within the Grasslands. Managed by the Forest Service in the Department of Agriculture, these federal Grasslands are largely badlands, intermingled with much private land that is more productive. However, there are large blocks of contiguous public land (Map 7.2)[4], and these could be expanded with land trades and, in time, purchases from willing sellers. A barrier to expanding bison range onto the Grasslands is the entrenched cattle industry with grazing leases on the public lands. Free-ranging bison would require a reduction of private livestock. A second, related barrier is the State. North Dakota does not recognize bison as a native wildlife species.

Major Ecotypes of Wild Plains Bison

Map 7.1. The Charles M. Russell National Wildlife Refuge (black) is a large area of prairie surrounding Fort Peck Reservoir. It is surrounded by a large amount of other federal multiple-use land managed by the Bureau of Land Management (gray) and some state land (also gray). In this large area, there is a modicum of private land (white), including some bison-friendly private land owned by the American Prairie Reserve (also black).

(Ironically, the North Dakota commemorative quarter depicts bison, as does the North Dakota license plate!) Do the people of North Dakota accept two penned bison herds in the National Park, managed much as livestock, to be as close as they will come to having wild bison in their state?

Fig. 7.2. With declining human populations, many small towns of the Great Plains have fallen on hard economic times. These buildings stand in a town that is a Montana county seat.

Fig. 7.3. Much of the land in Badlands National Park is poor or mediocre bison habitat, devoid of vegetation.

114

Major Ecotypes of Wild Plains Bison

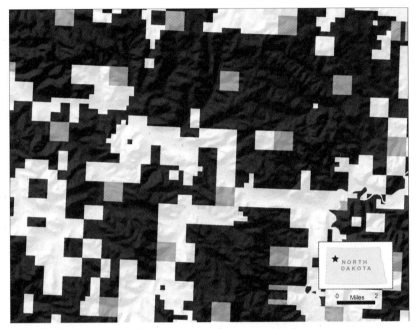

Map 7.2. Portion of Little Missouri National Grassland illustrating the proportions of public and private land. Public lands are federal, multiple-use lands (black) managed by the Forest Service and state lands (gray).Private lands (white) are interspersed.

Also, a large and mostly public bison range could be established in southwest South Dakota. The core areas would be Badlands National Park, which has bison, and the Buffalo Gap National Grassland. Some public land is adjacent to the Pine Ridge Indian Reservation, which might cooperate in establishing and maintaining a wild bison herd. Much of the National Grassland is fragmented and intermingled with private land, but there are some large contiguous blocks of federal Grassland adjacent to the Park (Map 7.3).[4] Judicious land trading and acquisition could be used to block up a bison range. Private livestock would have to be reduced or removed from some

115

public land. A limitation of this area for bison is that much of the land is relatively barren badlands (Fig. 7.3), and there will be a continuing tendency to relegate bison to the poorest lands because these will be easiest to acquire.

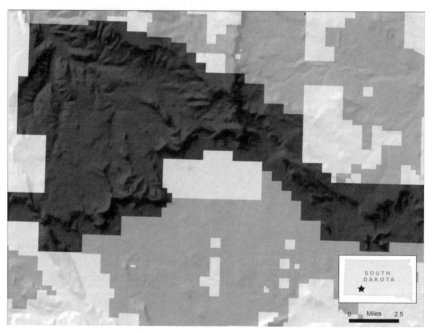

Map 7.3. Portion of Badlands National Park (black) including an area with 600 bison. The Park is surrounded by other public federal land (National multiple-use Grassland, gray) with better bison habitat and by private land (white).

Other areas of the northern Great Plains that should be analyzed as possible wild bison habitat are the Custer National Forest in southeast Montana and the Thunder Basin National Grassland in Wyoming. However, in the latter area, public lands are highly fragmented and very much intermingled with private lands.

Central Great Plains Bison

In the central Great Plains, wild bison may be restored somewhere in Nebraska, Kansas, southeast Wyoming or eastern Colorado. However, bison are not recognized as wildlife in state laws for any of this area.

While blizzards may occur, the central Great Plains have milder winters compared to the northern plains. The record low temperature is minus 47 degrees F; but winter warm spells are common, especially southward. Chinook winds occasionally warm and dry eastern Colorado during winter. Deep, persistent snow is rare. The tradeoff for milder winters is somewhat hotter and drier summers. Maximum recorded temperature in Kansas is 121 degrees F. Drought years are common, especially in the semi-arid west. Annual precipitation varies from about 40 inches in southeast Kansas to 14 inches in west Nebraska and east Colorado.

Topographic diversity of the central Great Plains includes much rolling and hilly grassland in the eastern half of the region. Extensive sand hills with easily eroded soil in north-central Nebraska are unique in North America. To the south are the Smoky Hills and Flint Hills of Kansas. Westward, there are badlands and the conifer-laden Pine Ridge in northwest Nebraska. Major rivers flowing eastward are the Platte, Arkansas, Niobrara, Republican, Kansas and Smoky Hill. There are also hundreds of smaller, sometimes intermittent streams.

As with the other Great Plains regions, central Plains vegetation grades from tallgrass prairie in the east, through mixed-grass prairie to short grasses in the west.

Establishing a large public grassland, with bison, in the Central Plains could benefit and conserve very many grassland species that are rare or have been declining. Notable species are listed in Table 7.1.

Rural human populations have been declining in the central Plains for a century. In Nebraska, 53 counties, mostly in the west, lost population during 1990-2000. Kansas has about 6000 ghost towns and declining communities. Baca County in southeast Colorado lost

16% of its population during 2000-2010 and now supports fewer than 2 people per square mile.

Eight conservation herds of plains bison in the Central Plains are: Niobrara Valley Preserve, TNC, NE (500 bison); Fort Robinson State Park, NE (500); Fort Niobrara National Wildlife Refuge, NE (350); Konza Prairie, KS (275); Maxwell State Wildlife Refuge, KS (165); Tallgrass Prairie National Preserve, KS (100); Rocky Mountain Arsenal National Wildlife Refuge, CO (55); and Sandsage Preserve, KS (20). (TNC = The Nature Conservancy.) Each of these herds has severe limitations for maintaining wild plains bison, as discussed in Chapter 11.

Kansas and eastern Nebraska have no large area of public land that might serve as a core for developing a large grassland preserve. Western Nebraska has the McKelvie and Nebraska National Forests, Crescent Lake National Wildlife Refuge and the Oglala National Grassland. Colorado has the Pawnee and Comanche National Grasslands. Lands near to or within the boundaries of one or more of these federal properties could be consolidated over time by trades or purchases from willing sellers – to establish a large contiguous area for plains bison and other prairie wildlife.

However, there has been much local and regional opposition to even considering such federal projects in the past. Federal lands noted above are mostly areas of mediocre soils in areas that have seen declining livestock-based economies for almost a century. Today, these areas survive on federal subsidies, including low grazing fees for using public lands. Opposing a large public grassland preserve will not stop the century-long downward economic trend in the western Central Plains. In contrast, diversifying the economy with recreation-based income based on a grassland preserve would benefit local communities, and provide a future for wild plains bison and other prairie wildlife.

Strategic analysis of potential sites for a large grassland/plains bison preserve should not be limited to areas in and surrounding current federal reservations. Large areas of federal land usually have poor soils that would support mediocre grasslands and mediocre bison herds. Perhaps better opportunities for the future of plains bison exist elsewhere. A former U.S. senate candidate espoused establishing a million-acre Great Plains national park in the two least populated counties of Kansas.[6] (Wallace County, with 1485 people, declined by 15% during 2000-2010. Greeley County, with 1247 people, declined by 19%.) Then there is the huge Cherry County, Nebraska, with an average human population of 1 person/sq. mile. In such areas, lands for a grassland/plains bison preserve could be accumulated gradually from willing sellers. But it will not happen if we never get started.

Southern Great Plains Bison

The Great Plains end in central Texas. To the south are desert grasslands and shrublands in Texas and Mexico. These arid lands once supported relatively sparse herds of plains bison, but are not considered here.

In the southern Great Plains, wild bison may be restored somewhere in Oklahoma, eastern New Mexico, or northwest Texas. Of the three states, Oklahoma law does not recognize bison as wildlife.

Continued global warming will limit the biological capacity of this region for bison restoration. However, the deteriorating climate may also reduce the already declining economic value of livestock grazing in at least some areas, reducing or eliminating competition for land needed to restore native grassland and bison. How this will play out is quite uncertain.

Summers are long and usually quite hot in the southern Great Plains. While the extreme high temperature, 120 degrees F, is essentially the same as in the northern and central Plains, there are many more hot days in the southern Plains. Parts of Oklahoma have seen years with up to 35 days having temperatures exceeding 100 F. Winters are generally mild with few, brief periods of cold. Average annual precipitation varies greatly from over 50 inches in southeast Oklahoma to 15 inches in east New Mexico. Most precipitation falls in summer. Winters tend to by dry. Episodes of drought may last several years. The drought of 1930-1940 involved the famous Dust Bowl.

The southern Great Plains tend to be hilly and rolling in the east and nearly flat in most of the west. Major topographic features include The Wichita Mountains in southwest Oklahoma and the elevated, flat-topped and arid Llano Estacado of west Texas and east New Mexico. The east and west boundaries of the Llano, or Caprock, area have eroded into minor canyons providing a modicum of topographic diversity. Major rivers are the Canadian and the Red. Many lesser rivers may not run year-round. Locally, canyons such as Palo Duro Canyon in Texas and the Canadian River Canyon in New Mexico add more topographic diversity. In the west, numerous playa lakes provide unique wildlife habitats that, no doubt, were once used by bison. These ephemeral wetlands limit opportunities for on-site agriculture but are important sources of recharge for the southern plains aquifer.

In the southern Great Plains, tallgrass prairie is limited to northeast Oklahoma. Most of the grasslands are either mixed-grasses to the east or short grasses to the west. Eastward and southward, there is tree encroachment onto the grasslands by oak and cedar. Fire is the common mediator of this competition between grassland and woodland. A unique form of low-growing oak, shinnery, is common on sandy sites westward, especially on the Llano Estacado. With only modest topographic diversity, the prevailing aridity is a major factor limiting habitat variation on most of these grasslands.

Prominent grasses of the southern mixed grass prairie are little bluestem, side-oats grama, and Indiangrass. More than half the mixed grass prairie has been converted to cropland and other uses. Westward, are the short grasses: blue grama, buffalograss, hairy grama and galleta. Western wheat grass occupies wetter sites, particularly around playa lakes. Prickly pear cactus, yucca and snakeweed are also common.

Among the many declining grassland animal species, several could benefit from a large grassland preserve in the southern Great Plains

Major Ecotypes of Wild Plains Bison

(Chart 7.1).

The rural population of the southern Great Plains has been declining for decades. Many small towns are in decline. Several counties have between fewer than 1 and 5 people per square mile. Harding County, New Mexico had but 695 citizens in 2010, having declined by 30% during the last 20 years. Regionally, the major rural income is from livestock production, struggling with recurring droughts. Creating a recreation based attraction of a grassland reserve with wild bison and other wildlife could add both diversity and stability to local and regional economies.

There are but four conservation herds of plains bison in the Southern Plains: Tallgrass Prairie Preserve in eastern OK, TNC, (1950 bison); Wichita Mountains National Wildlife Refuge, OK, (650); Clymer Meadows, TX, TNC (320); and Caprock State Park, TX (62). In recent decades, New Mexico denied its public trust responsibility for two small bison herds on non-native range in the west half of the state. One herd was on a small military base that was being decommissioned. New Mexico first proposed to eliminate the herd with public shooting, but then facilitated transfer of these bison to Native Americans. Other bison were an international herd in the southwest corner of New Mexico. These were allowed to be fenced and privatized within the state.

The only relatively large areas of mostly contiguous federal land in these southern Great Plains are the Kiowa and Rita Blanca National Grasslands in northeast New Mexico and the Texas panhandle.

In north Texas, the Rita Blanca Grassland has a block of over 50 square miles of contiguous public land. It is surrounded by very many disconnected small public tracts, some in Oklahoma, that might be traded to enlarge the current core public area. Additional lands could be purchased as they become available from willing sellers. Areas with large playa lakes should be a priority.

In New Mexico, the Kiowa National Grassland has no comparable large core area of contiguous federal land upon which to accumulate a large grassland reserve. Federal lands are more interspersed with private and some state land. However, an area from the Canadian River (Mills) Canyon eastward, mostly in Harding County north of the town of Roy, has more than 60 square miles of federal land that is about 50% of the landscape (Map 7.4).[4] With long-term public commitment, using land trades and purchases from willing sellers, at least 100 square miles of contiguous grassland reserve, with public bison, could be assembled. Within such a reserve, inholdings of state land would most likely be traded for outlying areas of federal land, as these state lands must be used to generate annual incomes for the state school system.

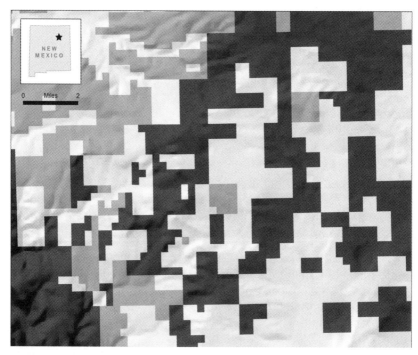

Map 7.4. Federal public multiple-use land (Kiowa National Grassland (black), north of Roy, in northeast New Mexico. The intervening land is state (gray) and private (white).

Elsewhere, there are large areas of private, sparsely inhabited land along the Canadian River in the Texas panhandle. Perhaps a long-term pubic/private effort could assemble a public grassland reserve in one of these areas. Is Texas big enough, geographically and otherwise, to restore a large herd of wild bison?

If public wild bison are to be returned anywhere in the southern Great Plains, the citizens of New Mexico, Texas, and possibly Oklahoma will have to demonstrate strong public support for their reintroduction. Currently, Oklahoma does not recognize bison as wildlife and New Mexico has recently demonstrated its ability to ignore bison as wildlife.

Mountain Bison

I include the mountains of the Colorado Plateau with the Rocky Mountains as the range of this bison ecotype. This is the largest and most diverse potential bison range, extending 950 miles and 13 degrees of latitude from Canada to northern New Mexico, and including parts of Montana, Idaho, Wyoming, Utah and Colorado. Among these states, Colorado law does not recognize bison as wildlife.

The area has great, topographic diversity, as elevation, aspect, slope, microclimate, soils and resulting vegetation vary across short distances. Whereas we believe bison of the Great Plains once traveled across hundreds of miles to access temporarily favorable environments, bison of the Rocky Mountains could accomplish as much by traveling over a few hundred feet of elevation.

Across the region, and locally, climatic variation is extreme. Mountains exceed 14,000 feet in Colorado. The lowest recorded temperature has been -61 degrees F at Maybell, Colorado. Precipitation varies greatly with aspect and elevation, from less than 15 inches to more than 40 inches per year. Many areas experience deep, long-lasting snow that precludes year-round occupation by bison.

Mountain grasslands must have been the core bison range. These varied from alpine grasslands at elevations above treeline, to meadows of all sizes within the mid-elevation forested zones, to wide, open valleys called "parks" in the south and "holes" in the north. Periodic fires once enlarged and maintained these grasslands. With the great diversity of ecological conditions, very many grass species were available to bison: fescue, wheatgrass, needlegrass, muhlygrass, bluegrass, grama grass, junegrass and oat grass among others.

Bison once exploited all these grasslands (Chapter 2). They would have used shrub-steppes that occurred in drier locations, and open forests with ponderosa pines or junipers, to a lesser extent. However, early records provide little information regarding seasonal use of habitats by bison in the Rocky Mountains. Likely, several large valleys such as South Park in Colorado, the Valley of the Three Forks in Montana, the upper Snake River Valley in Idaho and the upper Green River basin in Wyoming supported the largest herds that maintained most of the regional bison genome.

Today, these large mountain grasslands, particularly in wide valleys or parks, tend to be the most developed areas of the Rocky Mountain landscape. Most large valleys are bisected by a major highway and often a railroad. Large areas are flooded by reservoirs that are surrounded by recreational housing. Productive soils have been converted to dryland or irrigated farming or tame hay production. There is very little public land in the valleys where most habitat is intensively managed for agriculture or livestock - industries that support towns in the valleys.

Species of concern that could benefit from establishing a mountain grassland reserve with wild bison include grizzly bear, gray wolf, pygmy rabbit, white-tailed prairie dog, sage grouse, long-billed curlew, burrowing owl, Columbian sharp-tailed grouse, Gunnison's sage grouse, northern leopard frog, westslope cutthroat trout and arctic grayling.

In contrast to the Great Plains, most counties in the Rocky Mountain region experienced increasing human populations during 2000-2010. The area's abundance of public land, mostly at the higher elevations, accounts for much of the attraction. During the decade, many counties grew by 10-35% and more. Very few counties had static populations. This strong economic and population growth will deter any possible expansion or reestablishment of bison in the intermountain valleys where most people live and intensively use the land.

There are eight conservation herds of plains bison within the Mountains: Yellowstone National Park, WY/MT/ID (3700 bison); Medano Ranch, CO, TNC (2000); Jackson Valley, WY (500); Henry Mountains, UT (350); National Bison Range, MT (350); Book Cliffs, UT (100, with a goal of 450); Denver Genesee Park, CO (34); and Denver Daniels Park, CO (28). The first two of these herds are the largest conservation herds of plains bison on native range in the USA. But neither herd occupies optimum bison habitat.

While the Yellowstone bison herd is very important and extremely valuable for restoring wild plains bison today, it originated as a relict, outlier herd within the once large and widespread Rocky Mountain bison population. Most of the Yellowstone herd is limited year-round to high elevation habitat. In some years, foraging and travel are limited by deep snow. There are important winter/spring big-game ranges outside the Park and a large portion of the bison herd tries to access these areas to avoid deep snows of late winter and to use early forage greenup at lower elevations. However, due to a very small risk of disease transmission from bison to cattle, and out of deference to the livestock industry, bison are allowed only minimal time and space outside Yellowstone Park. Bison may access winter/spring ranges just outside the Park for a short time in some years. Over 1,000 "excess" bison leaving the Park were sent to slaughter in 2008. Up to 700 were penned and fed within the Park in 2011. The herd is hazed back into the Park each May. Currently, the possibilities of relaxing, or intensifying, these restrictions in Montana are being discussed by the public and by federal and state agencies.

Our second largest conservation herd, at The Nature Conservancy's

Rewilding Plains Bison

Medano Ranch, lives with long, cold winters at about 7,000 feet elevation in the flat San Luis Valley, Colorado. Most of the vegetation is arid shrub-steppe with greasewood and rabbitbrush. The habitat is rather uniform and not optimum for bison. Medano bison concentrate on patches of grasses and sedges on artesian meadows within the shrub-steppe. The bison have a high rate of introgression with cattle genes. There is discussion of expanding the range of this herd to include adjacent lands with similar habitat in Great Sand Dunes National Park and on the Baca National Wildlife Refuge. Replacing the herd with pure bison is part of this discussion. Unfortunately, the proposed expansion of this herd's range would provide little, if any, new habitat diversity at different elevations, and the Baca Refuge is facing exploratory drilling for oil and gas.

The least intensively managed conservation herd of bison in the contiguous USA is in the Henry Mountains of Utah. Yet, there are severe limitations to its wildness. This herd, controlled by hunting, is not large and is threatened by inbreeding and loss of genetic diversity. Its habitat is a large, elevated island surrounded by semi-desert. Some of its grasslands are maintained with prescribed fire and mechanical removal of woody vegetation. There are no effective bison predators except perhaps an occasional mountain lion.

The Jackson Valley bison herd lives with severe mountain winters. It is maintained with supplemental feeding that is intended for elk on the National Elk Refuge. There were 1000 bison in 2011; but Wyoming is committed to reducing the herd to 500. These bison share range with wolves and grizzly bears. However, with so many vulnerable elk concentrated on feedgrounds in winter, there appears to be little predation on bison. Management of the Jackson Valley bison herd is entangled with economic interests that demand continuing the elk feedground, despite its role in facilitating disease transmission among the concentrated elk and the ominous predictions of a serious dieoff. Short-term economic self interests so constrain management of this bison herd that there is little hope that it may contribute much to restoring wild bison in the near future.

The National Bison Range, Montana, has one of our most prominent conservation herds. Regulated at 325-350 animals by annual roundups and selective culling, these bison are at risk of inbreeding and must be losing genetic diversity with genetic drift. They are managed much like livestock with forced rotations through fenced pastures. No predation has been noted.

While the Mountain bison herds include the two largest and two wildest herds on native range in the USA, no Mountain herd occupies any of the large intermountain grasslands that once supported the largest numbers of bison.

True restoration of the Mountain ecotype of wild bison will require a landscape where bison may seasonally access a variety of habitat types across a considerable elevation gradient. Despite the size and wildness of a few Mountain bison herds today, we do not have this kind of high-quality bison range in the Mountains.

For reestablishing a wild Mountain bison herd that would range across a large elevation gradient and have access to some large areas of intermountain grassland, the most obvious opportunity exists with the Yellowstone Park herd. At lower elevation, outside the Park, there are public lands, and private lands where bison are welcome. Bison have tried to access these areas. However, the most prominent issue is the minimal threat of brucellosis disease-transmission to livestock. Perhaps 25-30% of Yellowstone bison are infected with *Brucella* bacteria, which cause brucellosis in bison, cattle and other hoofed animals. However, bison have not been known to transmit *Brucella* to cattle in field conditions. Cases of brucellosis in cattle in the Yellowstone area have all been traced as almost certainly originating in the greater Yellowstone elk herd that is much more numerous and widespread than are bison. Much of the land that bison could use adjacent to Yellowstone Park has no cattle, and some has no cattle during the season when *Brucella* might be transmitted by cattle contact with infected, aborted bison fetuses or placentas. All that we know indicates that the risk of *Brucella* transfer from bison to cattle in this area is small and manageable. Yet, strong opposition to reestablishing wild bison outside the Park comes from the Montana livestock industry.

Bison in the Far West

West of the Rocky Mountains, there are opportunities for bison restoration in the Great Basin and on the Columbia River Plateau. Bison were rare or absent in most of this country at the time of European contact (Chapter 2). Bison may be restored somewhere in eastern Washington, eastern Oregon, northeast California, southwest Idaho, northern Nevada or Utah. However, Washington, Oregon, Nevada and California do not legally recognize bison as a wildlife species.

There are four reasons to restore a Far West ecotype of plains bison: (1) Historical and archeological evidence indicates that bison occurred west of the Rocky Mountains in recent times, and ecological evidence suggests that Native Americans contributed to their limited numbers and distribution – thus they may be considered "native" wildlife of the western states. It is arbitrary to propose that bison are native where they were eliminated by human efforts after European contact, but are non-native where they were eliminated by humans shortly before contact. (2) There is no reason to suggest that bison cannot persist in this area, much of which supports domestic cattle and some wild horses today. (3) The region contains huge areas of contiguous public land that should be occupied by public wildlife. (4) Without a far west herd of wild plains bison, the large human population along the west coast must travel about 1000 miles to see, enjoy and use wild plains bison.

Most of the Great Basin and Columbia Plateau is considered a cold desert. It is the driest region for bison restoration. Many areas average only 7 inches of precipitation per year, with most of this falling in the relatively cold winter and spring seasons. Winter precipitation with hot dry summers favors shrubs such as sagebrush, and limits herbaceous growth. Maximum summer temperatures are well over 100 degrees, yet record low temperatures are about minus 50 F.

A basin and range topography dominates most of the Great Basin. Expansive valleys are interspersed with large mountain ranges, providing a great deal of topographic diversity with level plains, rolling hills, alluvial fans and rugged uplands and canyons. Major rivers are the Humboldt, Owyhee, Snake and Columbia.

Lower elevations of this region are dominated by sagebrush steppe. Sparse grasses include needle grasses, wild rye, squirreltail and rice grass. With a past of excessive cattle grazing, much land has been invaded by non-native cheat grass, a poor forage during most of the year. In contrast, mountain slopes support stands of juniper woodland, mountain shrubland and open conifer forests. Wetlands are scarce and many are ephemeral evaporation basins.

Rare or declining wildlife species that could be enhanced by establishing a far-western grassland reserve with wild bison include: burrowing owl, ferruginous hawk, Swainson's hawk, golden eagle, prairie falcon, sage grouse, loggerhead shrike, snowy plover, kit fox and pygmy rabbit.

Most of this region is sparsely populated. The majority is federal land managed by the Bureau of Land Management, the Forest Service and other federal agencies. Most of this federal land is leased for seasonal livestock grazing.

The only conservation herd of plains bison on native far-western range is on Antelope Island State Park in the Great Salt Lake, with about 500 bison. With an adult sex ratio of 1 bull per 3 cows, the herd produces about 200 calves annually. Yearly roundups facilitate vaccinations and vermicide treatments, and the sale of animals to fund operations.

More than elsewhere, bison restoration in the Far West should begin with a commitment to provide a large, diverse landscape for eventual bison occupation. This is necessary because: (1) The region is quite arid with low forage production, thus requiring a large bison range to sustain a genetically sufficient number of animals. (2) Having almost no historical evidence of bison habitat-use in this area, we cannot predict how bison will use the landscape to meet their needs in all seasons and weather conditions. Lacking an ability to predict bison habitat, we should allow the animals to show us how they will best use the landscape. Utah's experience in introducing free-ranging bison into a shrub-steppe habitat, only to have the animals move permanently into the Henry Mountains, illustrates the dilemma.

I am less familiar with the Far West, compared to other regions that could support restoration of wild bison. With vast areas of sparsely populated and mostly public land, many areas should be analyzed as possibilities for bison. However, a cursory review of the region suggests two areas that may have good opportunities for bison restoration because they include federal wildlife refuges with wetlands to provide dry-season forage and are surrounded by abundant other federal land.

Ruby Lake National Wildlife Refuge, Nevada was established in 1938 "for migratory birds and other wildlife". It is surrounded mostly by extensive federal lands (Map 7.5).[4] There are higher elevations in the Ruby Mountains of the National Forest to the west, and vast areas of sagebrush steppe on Bureau of Land Management land to the south and east. The refuge could serve as a core area to learn how wild bison would use the available habitat diversity. Eventually, most of the northeast third of Nevada probably could support an immense population of wild bison, at low average density, on mostly public land.

Malheur National Wildlife Refuge, Oregon provides a similar opportunity for restoring wild bison. There is extensive BLM land south of both Harney and Malheur Lakes, connecting with the Hart Mountain National Wildlife Refuge (Map 7.6).[4] Numerous finds of bison skulls and bones, and Native American oral histories, demonstrate that this area supported bison in late-prehistoric or early-historic time (Chapter 2).

Major Ecotypes of Wild Plains Bison

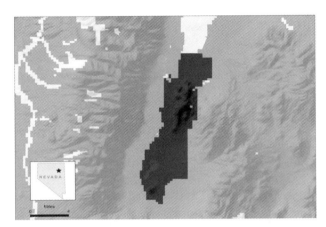

Map 7.5. In Nevada, Ruby Lakes National Wildlife Refuge (black) is surrounded by a vast area of other federal public, multiple-use land managed by the Bureau of Land Management and Forest Service (gray). There is very little private land (white).

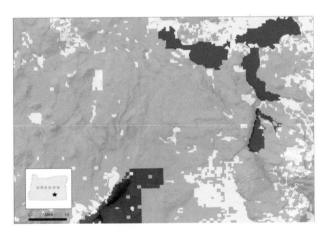

Map 7.6. Mostly federal multiple-use land (gray) and some state land (also gray) surrounding Malheur Lakes National Wildlife Refuge (black, northeast) and Hart Mountain National Wildlife Refuge (black, southwest).

131

Footnotes:

[1] Gates et al. (2010), p. 18.

[2] Sanderson et al. (2008).

[3] Popper and Popper (1987).

[4] The area partly depicted in Map 7.1 has no peer among locations in the USA with abundant federal land and good bison habitat, much already dedicated to wildlife. However, the areas depicted in Maps 7.2–7.6 are presented only as examples of many areas with abundant federal land that should be analyzed for possible plains bison restoration. Details are purposely omitted from these latter maps to avoid easy identification of anyone's private property.

[5] Manning (2009).

[6] News release of candidate Charles Schollenberger, June 25, 2010.

Chapter 8

Domestication of Plains Bison

In north-central Montana, the American Prairie Reserve is accumulating land and public grazing allotments to reestablish wild plains bison on native prairie. In 2011, APR had about 200 wild bison. During a recent cold winter, a local rancher accused APR of cruelty to animals. The rancher was providing supplementary hay to his cattle; whereas APR was not feeding hay to its bison. The rancher assumed the bison were starving; as his own cattle would have suffered without intervention. "But our bison were doing fine," said Jeff Hagener of APR. [1]

Similarly, on the Triple U Ranch in South Dakota, Roy Houck was unable to feed his stock, cattle and a few bison, for days during a severe snowstorm. When the storm finally ceased, many cattle were dead, but the bison were running and frolicking in the snow.[2]

These incidents illustrate one value of wildness in bison. They can take care of themselves, given adequate native forage and access to a diversity of natural habitat types. It also illustrates the common lack of awareness of the vast difference between wild and domestic animals and of the threat of domestication to wild plains bison.

Domestication can overtake bison just as it did the wild aurochs of the Old World.[3] Aurochs are ancestors of today's domestic cattle; but they no longer exist, except as pictographs in stone-age caves. The captive form of aurochs was altered and elaborated by human intervention, while the wild form was eliminated. At least 10 other species of large grazing mammals face this same demise. The Asian elephant, Dromedary and Bactrian camels, Yak, African wild ass, Asian wild horse, and four species of cattle (Zebu, Banteng, Gaur and Asian water buffalo) are numerous in domestication, but uncommon or rare in the wild (Fig. 8.1).

Control is a part of human nature. We try to control our environment; we try to control each other. Control brings safety, at least in the short term. Control brings the comfort of predictability. And so we domesticate what we can of the world's fauna and flora. We are on

Fig. 8.1. Six of the 10 large grazing mammals that are abundant in domestication but uncommon or rare in the wild: Asian elephant, banteng, Bactrian camel ...

Fig. 8.1. continued: Asian water buffalo, yak and gaur.

our way to domesticating bison – to the extinction of wild bison, at least south of Canada.

Much of the difference between a wild and a domesticated animal is seen in comparing a Yellowstone bison to a domestic cow. We know that bison use upland areas and steeper slopes more than do cattle. But, just looking at bison and cattle, there is no comparison. The bison is designed by natural selection to be strong, mobile, agile, fast, independent, competitive and wary. The domestic cow is designed by human selection to be calm, slow, tractable, directing as much energy as possible to producing body tissue, rather than to activity, and dependent upon humans to provide emergency food, to control diseases and perhaps to assist at birthing time.

But these obvious differences fail to demonstrate all that is unique and valuable in wildness, as opposed to the domesticated state. In domestication, what will happen to bison's acuity of sight, hearing, taste and scent? Bison are not known to have sharp eyesight, but their other senses appear keen. Without predators, the value of and selection for acute senses will be diminished.

Foraging wild deer are known to use taste and smell to detect minute plant differences in amounts and types of volatile oils that would hinder digestion.[4] Bison likely have similar abilities. But, in a limited bison pasture without a diversity of forages, selection for this ability to discriminate will decline.

The Wildness – Domestication Continuum

Wildness is the opposite of domestication. There is a continuum of conditions between the extremes of totally wild and totally domesticated. The benchmark of domestication is the degree of replacement of natural selection by artificial selection. Artificial selection, a term used by Charles Darwin, occurs when human decisions, conscious or unconscious, directly or indirectly, determine which animals survive and reproduce to leave their genes in the next generation.

Domestication of Plains Bison

In a wild population, natural selection in a natural environment is the preponderant mechanism determining which animals survive and reproduce. The more we intervene to manage wild populations, the more artificial selection will occur. Populations will adapt to us rather than to a wild, natural environment. They will be pushed along the continuum from wildness toward domestication.

Conservation biologists have recognized this continuum of wildness to domestication. They suggest five population "stages" to illustrate the continuum: 1) self-sustaining, 2) conservation dependent, 3) lightly managed, 4) intensively managed, and 5) captive managed.[5]

Human Interventions Leading to Domestication

Human interventions, replacing or weakening natural selection and resulting in domestication of wild bison, are listed below.

- Small herd sizes.

- Small herd ranges with little habitat diversity.

- Rotation through seasonal pastures.

- Intensive range/habitat manipulation.

- Provision of artificial waters.

- Supplementary feed during winter or drought.

- Annual roundups and selective culling (Figs. 8.2, 8.3).

- Selection of bulls for breeding.

- Control of breeding season by separating bulls and cows.

- Early, forced weaning of calves.

- Assistance in calving.

- Maintaining stable herd sizes well below ecological carrying capacity.

- Maintaining herds with unnaturally young age distributions.
- Maintaining an unnaturally low bull/cow ratio.
- Culling feisty, excitable, intractable bison.
- Unintentional injuries and deaths of excitable bison during handling (Fig. 8.4).
- Use of vaccinations, vermicides and antibiotics.
- No effective predators.

Fig. 8.2. Bison being processed during the annual roundup, Custer State Park, SD.

Fig. 8.3 The Custer State Park conservation herd of bison is rounded up and processed for handling and culling annually.

Fig. 8.4. Ear tags diminish esthetic value of wild bison. Broken and deformed horns are a common result from frequent handling of bison in pens and chutes. Effects of such deformities on dominance behavior of bison are uncertain.

The degree and rate of domestication will depend upon the number of these interventions being applied to a bison herd. Interventions will be most active in replacing natural selection when applied to young breeding-age animals, before natural selection has been allowed to operate. (But see section on Public Hunting in Chapter 12 for more on this complex topic.)

Perhaps no herd, not even the most commercial private herd, is subject to all these practices. But most bison herds, including those in the care of our state and federal wildlife agencies, are affected by many of these activities.[6] Even the bison of Yellowstone National Park, under the Interagency Bison Management Plan, are impacted by several interventions. Yellowstone bison are culled in a non-random manner. Herd size is limited. The average age of Yellowstone bison has been artificially reduced. Yellowstone bison have been vaccinated. During the winter of 2011, about 700 bison were held and fed in crowded pens for up to 4 months (Fig 8.5). Some of the most aggressive or nomadic individuals have been selectively shot. Access to seasonal ranges has been denied. And yet, Yellowstone has the wildest remaining herd of plains bison on native range in the USA!

Fig. 8.5. "Wild" bison being fed in holding pens within Yellowstone National Park during 2011 when up to 700 bison were retained for up to 4 months to prevent them from leaving the Park. (Buffalo Field Campaign photo)

Results of Human Interventions in Domesticating Bison

Domestication causes a slow dismantling of the adaptive syndrome that is wild bison. Genetic and some non-genetic impacts of domestication upon wild bison may include those listed below, although this list must underestimate effects.[7]

- Inbreeding, with negative effects on survival and reproduction.
- Loss of genetic diversity and ability to evolve and adapt to changing environments.
- Altered body size, smaller or larger, depending upon selection.
- Reduced skull and brain size.
- Diminished dominance behavior.
- Reduced nutritional and energetic efficiencies.
- Reduced maternal behavior, lower milk quality.
- Diminished ease of calving.
- Decline of precociousness in calves.
- Reduced synchrony of breeding and calving.
- Lethargy, less aggressiveness, reduced mobility and agility.
- Diminished disease resistance/accommodation.
- Reduced acuity of senses.
- Diminished ability to survive in the wild.

Some relationships between above human interventions and results in the bison genome are easy to comprehend. Others are more complex.

Traits are not always inherited independently. Those that tend to be inherited together are termed linked traits. For example, in a classic experiment, Russian scientist Dimitri Balyaev selectively removed animals from normally uniformly colored silver foxes in a fur farm. He culled the most aggressive animals and saved the tamest. In a few generations, Balyaev had, not only tame foxes, but animals with mottled fur, floppy ears and shorter tails!.[8]

In culling bison to limit herd sizes, managers often select aggressive, hard-to-handle animals for removal. Some managers, especially of commercial herds, also select smaller bison for sale, retaining the larger bison for breeding. Those that have grown most rapidly during their early years may be especially desired for subsequent breeding. This is exactly the process that has produced commercial, domestic cattle. Less excitable, more lethargic, less mobile and agile animals can divert more of their digested nutrients away from activity and into growth. This is a little recognized danger of selective culling in bison herds. Many characteristics of domestic animals can increase simultaneously as an unintended consequence.

Implications of non-random culling are seldom recognized. Often, the first bison to come through the handling chutes are chosen for removal. A Canadian study has shown that this approach emphasized removal of the largest animals.[9] Other bison traits probably are linked to body size and were being artificially selected unknowingly.

Even random culling of bison will weaken natural selection. Random removal of animals treats the most fit and least fit bison equally, whereas natural selection would favor survival and reproduction of bison most suited for wild conditions.

The role of disease control in wild bison is a difficult and controversial issue. Simplistically, we want our wild bison to be "healthy", yet wild ecosystems are anything but simple. The absence of pathogens in an ecosystem would be as unnatural as the absence of predators. However, several diseases of bison may be transmitted to domestic livestock.[10] These diseases are unwelcome threats to private interests, however small or manageable the threats may be. Adding to the difficulty and controversy, 1) a few diseases that may infect bison and other hoofed animals are rarely transmitted to humans; 2) some diseases are not native to North America so that bison and other wildlife have had relatively little evolutionary history with these pathogens; 3) some pathogens may persist undetectably in bison for years before becoming transmittable; and 4) several diseases that may infect bison are highly regulated by government agencies at all levels. Government pathologists often presume that methods of disease control developed with domestic livestock are appropriately and effectively applied to wildlife. Both presumptions are questionable.

At the extremes, there are two models for disease management for humans, for our domestic animals including livestock, and for our wildlife. These and their important characteristics, especially for wildlife management, are:

1. Intensive intervention and management of disease.

• Comparatively simple interventions with quarantines, culling infected animals, vaccinations, vermicides and antibiotics to produce quick, short-term benefits.

• When public issues are involved, interventions are especially attractive to political interests that are, by nature, short-term.

• Interventions may treat the most and least disease-resistant animals equally, thereby weakening any natural selection for resistance.

• Interventions create long-term commitments because animals fail to evolve resistance while pathogens evolve and adapt to the interventions, requiring constant development of new vaccines, antibiotics and other intervention techniques.

• Pharmaceutical and veterinary industries develop a strong financial and lobbying system for research and continued responsive intervention.

2. Mother Nature's time-tested model.

- Time-tested by centuries of evolution; animals develop resistance and evolve accommodation with pathogens that also evolve toward reduced virulence. (The rapid evolution of European hares and the myxoma virus in Australia exemplifies this coevolution.)

- May be costly in the short-term; much less costly in the long-term.

- Brutal system: animals die of disease as natural selection operates. However, some predators are skilled at detecting and quickly removing infected animals. Disease-debilitated animals are selectively disadvantaged as inferior competitors for resources and breeding.

- Relatively little public understanding of evolution and the complexities of animal physiology. ("Take a pill and call me in the morning." is so much easier to grasp!)

- Consequently, there is rather little public support for systems of natural regulation, as illustrated by the difficulty that our National Park Service has had in applying this approach.

We are clearly committed to intensive medical intervention for managing human disease, though not without setbacks including serious epidemics of Spanish, Hong Kong, Asian and bird flu and the recent rise of antibiotic-resistant bacteria. We are also committed to this model for our domestic animals and livestock, at considerable perpetual cost. Success in these two arenas has caused us to presume that the intervention model is also best for our wildlife. There has been too little discussion of the wisdom of this presumption and of the costs in lost values of wildness.

Intervention with selective culling, vaccines, antibiotics and vermicides may prevent, reduce or delay disease problems in wild bison. However, effects of these interventions may not be limited simply to one target pathogen and its host. All mammals carry hundreds of competing and synergistic species and strains of bacteria, viruses and other potential pathogens. These interact complexly with several biochemical and cell-mediated mechanisms of disease resistance. It seems unlikely that we can change one part of this complex micro-system without causing compensatory changes in other parts of the system.[11] With disease control, we are interfering with evolved and evolving mechanisms of resistance and accommodation between bison and their pathogens. We do not fully understand the implications of wildlife disease control; and we will not learn what they are unless we retain at least a few wild populations without disease control, as a basis for comparison.

Under natural selection, bison with the least disease resistance, or bison carrying the most virulent, debilitating strains of a pathogen, will experience relatively low rates of reproduction and/or survival. In this coevolving system, natural selection favors persistence of disease resistant bison and of less virulent strains of pathogens. The result is disease accommodation.[12] In reality, a sick animal is a natural component of a "healthy", evolving ecosystem.

In contrast, intervention with vaccines, antibiotics and vermicides can impede natural selection for resistance and accommodation. It may also cause loss of whatever disease resistance bison already carry. Intervention will be a commitment to continued human management to maintain susceptible bison that are obligated to humans for disease control. Disease management is domestication. Unfortunately, a recent review of principles for managing bison diseases ignored these issues and assumed that failure to intervene with bison diseases would be an "inappropriate management strategy".[13]

The issue of disease, especially of brucellosis, is exaggerated in public discussions of possible bison restoration. It is a serious issue because brucellosis and a few other diseases transmittable between bison and livestock may be economic burdens for the livestock industry. However, brucellosis has been used to prevent bison restoration by overstating the risks of transmission to livestock, even when uninfected bison are involved. This politically successful tactic has been used to avoid the embarrassing argument that public bison will compete with private livestock for public forage on public land. In contrast, a fair-minded approach would 1) consider the biological realities of bison/*Brucella* ecology; 2) equally recognize private property rights and public property rights; and 3) equally disclose and consider both public and private costs and benefits of any proposed bison restoration.

Predation has been a major selective force creating wild bison. Today, only two plains bison herds on native range in the USA – both in the Yellowstone area – live with effective predators. Removal of predators allows individuals with less acute senses to survive and reproduce. Without predators, there is less advantage for synchronous breeding and calving, for ease of calving, for precocious calves and for high-density milk to support rapid calf growth. Likewise, there is less selective pressure favoring mobility and agility and less selective removal of individuals that fail to develop adaptations for disease resistance.

Mate selection, with the dominance of large, agile bulls has been another major selective force in bison. In wild bison herds, most breeding is accomplished by bulls that are 8 or more years old. Dominant bulls have proven their abilities to survive, to resist debilitating diseases, to forage effectively and to digest forages efficiently in order to outcompete other bulls. Years of natural selection are represented in each dominant breeding bull. In many managed plains bison herds, this selection is lost as most bulls are culled at an early age based on human decisions, and bull competition is largely eliminated by maintaining a herd sex ratio of 1 bull per 10 or more adult cows (Chapter 11).

Moreover, there is evidence that female mammals, using the scent of prospective breeding males, can detect and consent to breed with males having different alleles from their own. This behavior thwarts inbreeding and enhances valuable genetic diversity in offspring. In bison, the common practice of running small herds with relatively few breeding-age males, or of selecting bulls for breeding, must obstruct this valuable component of natural sexual selection.

Periodic severe winters and droughts have always tested wild bison, selecting for energetic and digestive efficiencies. Persistence of these adaptations is compromised by supplemental feeding, pasture rotation, habitat/forage enhancement, and by maintaining bison herd sizes well below the ecological carrying capacities of their ranges. If no bison are dying on the ranges, natural selection is not working.

Relationships among human interventions that generate artificial selection and alter the bison genome are more complex and interrelated than these few obvious examples suggest. Reduced natural selection for aggressiveness and dominance behavior may result from at least 11 of the 18 interventions listed above. In turn, dominance enhances or mediates several other results of human interventions.

Many of these impacts, and others we do not expect, must be occurring in plains bison. While natural selection usually proceeds slowly, domestication in combination with genetic drift may cause rapid changes in the genetic composition of a population. How many generations are required for loss of wild characteristics to be obvious? We do not know; but it will depend on the intensity of human intervention into the natural-selection process. This intervention has begun. Almost all our plains bison have been under some level of domestication, mostly in small herds, for more than 100 years. Some impacts should be measurable already, if we would look carefully.

How far this may go is demonstrated by the very many breeds of domestic cattle and domestic dogs. Aurochs, the progenitor of cattle is extinct. However, wolves, the source of domestic dogs, continued in the wild on a separate evolutionary track while we were domesticating and selectively breeding dogs. Will wild plains bison go the way of aurochs, or of wolves? Knowingly or not, we are making that decision in bison management today.

Empirical evidence of domestication

Currently, the Yellowstone National Park bison are our only standard of wildness of plains bison. Only in Yellowstone have some plains bison persisted always as wild animals. Only in Yellowstone do significant numbers of bison live with large predators on native range. If we are to measure effects of domestication, or semi-domestication, upon bison – now or in the future – we must retain wildness in the Yellowstone herd as a basis for comparison.

Yet Yellowstone bison can provide a sample size of only one herd; and the Park is not the best possible habitat for retaining a sample of wild bison. Originally, this upper Yellowstone area supported a backwater population on the periphery of better plains bison habitat. It is a harsh habitat, at least at some seasons, for plains bison today. If we are to preserve examples of wild bison, we should do so in more than one place, and in some places with better bison habitat than Yellowstone National Park.

References:

[1] Personal communication, Jeff Hagener was executive director of the American Prairie Reserve during 2011.

[2] The Triple U Ranch experience was related at livestockrus.com.

[3] Gates et al. (2010) discuss the threat of domestication to conservation of the wild character and genome of bison.

[4] I participated in this research on forage selection by mule deer at Colorado State University.

[5] Redford et al. (2011).

[6] At the American Bison Society's conference in Tulsa, Oklahoma in 2011, biologists concluded "Artificial selection due to the way bison are managed has in various ways replaced natural selection among the vast majority of bison herds in North America, including herds managed primarily for conservation purposes."

[7] Effects of captivity and domestication on animals are summarized by Clutton-Brock(1999), O'Regan and Kitchener (2005) and references therein. The latter paper emphasizes effects of captivity in

cages, zoos and relatively small pens. In contrast, most bison herds in the USA live in pens of at least a few square miles. However, for bison, a species that evolved to be highly mobile and to use a diversity of habitats, we should expect the pen-size effects of captivity to be exacerbated.

[8] The Belyaev experiment is described by O'Regan and Kitchener (2005) and on line.

[9] Personal communication, Wes Olson, wildlife biologist, Grasslands National Park, Saskatchewan.

[10] Gates et al. (2010) review diseases that may infect bison. However, the website of the National Bison Association, an organization of commercial bison producers, touts the superior (to cattle) disease resistance of bison.

[11] Woolhouse et al. (2002) provide a useful review of many interrelated processes in coevolution of pathogens and their hosts.

[12] Meyer (1992) noted greater resistance of wild bison to *Brucella abortus*, causative agent of brucellosis, compared to resistance in domestic cattle. Seabury et al. (2005) detected evidence of a genetic basis for this resistance in Yellowstone bison. Either the resistance of bison to *Brucella* is a case of "preadaptation" or some resistance and accommodation evolved during about 10 generations of bison since first exposure of the Yellowstone herd.

[13] Nishi (2010).

Part III

American Plains Bison in the Modern Era

The brush with extinction is not over. For more than 100 years, we have been slowly domesticating plains bison, leading to extinction of the wild form.

Chapter 9

20th Century: From Devastation to Limbo

Brush with Extinction

The nadir of plains bison abundance occurred before 1900. Warnings of the decline towards extinction had been sounded much earlier by: Major Stephen Long, 1820; George Catlin 1832; John Audubon 1843; Josiah Gregg 1845; and William Hornaday 1875. These and other warnings were largely ignored. Fortunately, a few individuals and families collected bison calves to begin small private herds. Charles Goodnight of Texas gathered his first bison calves in 1866 and a Native American, Walking Coyote, tamed Montana bison calves in 1873. James McKay gathered a few Canadian plains bison, also in 1873. A Lakota family, the Dupree's, captured plains bison in 1881. The McCoy brothers of Oklahoma obtained bison in 1883; and C. J. "Buffalo" Jones obtained bison from Texas, Kansas and Nebraska and then bought plains bison from Canada in 1888.[1]

Shortly before the turn of the century, all or very nearly all the remaining plains bison in North America, probably fewer than 200, were in these six original private herds and the no more than 50 bison in Yellowstone National Park.[2] Unfortunately, most or all the six private owners either allowed or forced bison to breed with cattle, producing some fertile cows that were then bred back into the bison herds. Cattle-gene introgression began and spread.

Early Restoration Efforts

At first, privatization of plains bison grew rapidly. David Dary states that by 1902 there were more than 700 bison in an unknown number of private herds in the United States. The rapid increase from the low, "bottleneck" population probably saved much genetic diversity of plains bison. However, it was clear that private bison herds would not be a salvation for the species. Owners lost interest or died, and bison were sent to slaughter. Many owners continued to experiment in cross-breeding with cattle. No doubt, they all managed bison as livestock. In Yellowstone National Park, most bison were also managed this way.[2] The process of domestication began very early.

Government indifference led a few, mostly wealthy, eastern gentlemen to take up the cause of saving some semblance of wild bison for future generations.[3] Bison restoration started as a private enterprise. Ernest Baynes began to promote saving bison for future generations in 1904. He apparently influenced President Theodore Roosevelt to mention the plight of wild bison in his 1905 message to Congress. Baynes also stimulated formation of The American Bison Society in 1905. Prominent leaders of the Society were William Hornaday, director of the New York Zoological Park, Ernest Thompson Seton and Baynes. Theodore Roosevelt was honorary president. Membership of the Society grew to several hundred, mostly from large northeastern cities.

If the fate of bison had depended upon people who lived in the center of the continent, bison may not have survived. An eastern movement, augmented by the press, literary media, and art, elevated bison conservation to effective levels.

As described below, urging and participation from members of the American Bison Society accelerated federal efforts to preserve some plains bison. These efforts unintentionally continued the process of domesticating public bison. It is not surprising that the threat of domestication created little, if any, concern. It had been less than 50 years since Charles Darwin had published *On the Origin of Species,* so the important role of natural selection for maintaining wildness was rarely recognized and little understood.

Considering the influence of Darwin's ideas on the early life of Theodore Roosevelt, one must wonder if Roosevelt recognized, but pragmatically accepted, the domesticating implications of early attempts to restore plains bison.[4] He conceded the northern Great Plains bison habitat as "the northern cattle plains" (Hunting Trips of a Ranchman, 1885). Later, he envisioned saving a large buffalo commons (Forest & Stream, 1893). It is understandable that a young Roosevelt, in his early writings, would concentrate primarily on the issue of preventing wildlife destruction through unregulated commercial and "sport" harvest. The wasteful destruction of big game was everywhere obvious, while the more esoteric issues of habitat and, with it, disappearance of natural selection, were neglected in early wildlife conservation. While Roosevelt eventually recognized the importance of habitat, we are still grappling with the issue and importance of natural selection for maintaining wildness of our wildlife.

A Century of Warehousing Plains Bison

In 1905, the only wild bison – perhaps fewer than 30 – were in Yellowstone National Park. The Park had another 44 bison, mixed from Yellowstone, Texas and northern Montana sources, held like domestic livestock near Mammoth.[2] The only other federal bison were at the National Zoo in Washington, DC. In Yellowstone, most of the Mammoth bison were moved to the "Buffalo Ranch" in the Park's Lamar Valley in 1907. They continued to be managed as livestock for several years: herded and/or fenced in during the day; penned at night; and provided with supplemental feed from irrigated hay fields in the Park.

In 1907, 15 plains bison from the New York Zoo were transferred to what is now the Wichita Mountains National Wildlife Refuge in Oklahoma (Fig. 9.1). Congress had provided funds for fencing and to build corrals, handling chutes and sheds to manage these bison much as livestock.

In a similar 1909 effort, Congress established a National Bison Reserve in Montana, with 37 animals obtained from private sources, mostly purchased by the American Bison Society. Hornaday declared that bison were no longer in danger of extinction in 1911, but restoration efforts continued. In 1913, bison were established at Fort Niobrara, Nebraska and at Wind Cave National Game Preserve, South Dakota. Based on these four plains bison herds, plus the Yellowstone herd and a few other minor public herds, the American Bison Society began to consider its mission accomplished in 1915.

(However, the Society did not fully disband until 1935, only to be re-established in 2005.)

Fig. 9.1. In 1907, Bronx Zoo staff sent 15 bison by rail to Wichita Mountains Wildlife Preserve, Oklahoma. Photo courtesy of American Bison Society.

Early success in establishing fenced populations of plains bison was followed by several public and private initiatives with fenced (or island) populations of plains bison on limited ranges where they would be subjected to some degree of intensive management. In 1910, there were about 10 of these non-commercial "conservation" herds, owned by government agencies or by private conservation organizations. The number of these herds has grown steadily to about 64 conservation herds of plains bison in North America in 2010.[5]

In 1928, F. M. Fryxell noted that restoring wild bison "unmarred by fence or corral" was a possibility for which public sentiment and support could be enlisted.[6] Again in 1947, when there were about 20 conservation herds of plains bison, Victor Cahalane recognized the threat of domesticating wild bison as he wrote: "A big national monument should be established in the Great Plains area where a moderate sized herd could live under primitive conditions, together with other plains species. This would ensure the perpetuation of the animal as a wild species, free from the danger of domestication."[7] However, the ongoing threat of domesticating bison attracted little attention.

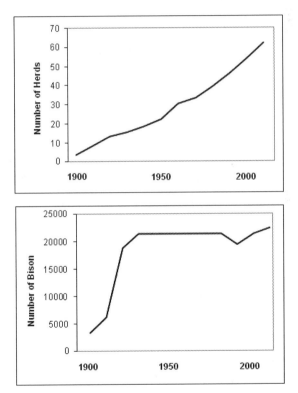

Chart 9.1. Increasing number of plains bison conservation herds (above) and numbers of conservation bison (below) in North America, 1900-2010; based on Gates et al. 2010.

Rewilding Plains Bison

While the number of conservation herds of plains bison has continued to grow, the number of bison within these herds has remained static at about 20,000 animals since 1930 (Chart 9.1). The implication is that average herd size has been declining. This is confirmed by the numerous small or very small conservation herds of plains bison today (Chart 11.1).

Meanwhile, the number of commercial herds and commercial bison grew gradually at first and rapidly after about 1960. The number of commercial bison first exceeded the number of conservation bison around 1970.[8] Today, 90% of plains bison are in private, commercial herds, almost all managed to maximize meat production (Chapter 10).

Now, there are 64 conservation herds of plains bison in North America.[5] However, only 44 are on native plains bison range in the USA. Characteristics and limitations of these herds are reviewed in Chapter 11. During most of the 20th century, issues of genetic diversity, ecological relations, cattle-gene introgression, and domestication of bison attracted little or no attention because:

• Concerns for genetic diversity in small wildlife populations first became prominent about 1980.

• Most research on the relations of plains bison to grassland ecosystems has been published since 1980.

• The issue of cattle introgression in bison caused elevated concern in the late 1990s with the onset of genetic analyses of bison.

• Despite Cahalane's admonition, cited above, the threat of creeping domestication of bison has only recently been appreciated by some plains bison managers. Discussion of the domestication issue had barely begun, late in the 20th century.

Genetic Implications. Bison restoration began with rather few animals as founders of the herds we now have. Most of these founders came from the Great Plains. Any genetic diversity associated with eastern bison, or with most of the Rocky Mountains and westward, was lost.

We do not know the magnitude or consequences of genetic diversity lost during the severe bottleneck of plains bison in North America.

Recent research suggests that a managed population of 2000-3000 plains bison will lose an estimated 5% of its alleles in each 100 years.[9] However, the first 100 years, and more, of plains bison restoration are in the past. During the 20th century, very few plains bison herds exceeded 1000 animals for even a few years. We must assume that more than 5% of plains bison genetic diversity has already been lost, due to having few founders and due to genetic drift during the 20th century.

*   *   *   *   *   *   *   *

Those who began restoring plains bison around 1900 had little or no awareness of these issues. Certainly, we owe them for initiating the restoration process. But, based on today's knowledge of genetics, ecology, natural selection and evolution, we know that restoration is far from finished. Worse, opportunities to restore plains bison on native range have diminished as more land has become more intensively used and developed. We realize that we have been warehousing plains bison, awaiting a time when knowledge, public awareness and public support might prompt restoration with some truly wild herds of plains bison on large grassland reserves.

Footnotes

[1] The complicated early history of saving the last few plains bison is recounted in Dary (1974), Geist (1991) and Zontek (2007).

[2] Meagher (1973) summarized the earliest counts of bison in Yellowstone National Park.

[3] Early bison conservation efforts are described by Dary (1974).

[4] T. R. Roosevelt's early embracing of Darwinism, and his vision of

bison conservation are described by Brinkley (2009).

[5] Freese et al. (2007) and Gates et al. (2010). The latter list 62 conservation herds of plains bison in 2010. However, I count the bison in the north and south pens at Theodore Roosevelt National Park as 2 herds, as they are managed separately. Also, Gates et al. do not include the new bison herd at Tallgrass Prairie National Preserve, Kansas.

[6] Fryxell (1928).

[7] Cahalane (1947).

[8] Freese et al. (2007).

[9] Perez-Figueroa (2010).

Chapter 10

21st Century: An Imitation of Wildness

States Disregard Wild Plains Bison

In the USA, primary responsibility for managing wildlife rests with the individual states. This responsibility is shared with the federal government for migratory birds, especially waterfowl. And when the states fail to maintain a wildlife species, the Endangered Species Act allows for federal control and interventions.

The unique history of bison never prompted states to recognize their responsibility for the species. We switched so quickly, over a few decades, from a policy of bison destruction to thoughts of restoration that state policies did not keep pace. Early federal reserves of relatively small, intensively managed, fenced herds suggested that such conservation efforts would suffice. A few states responded by establishing display herds in public parks, many of which were extremely small; merely outdoor zoos. Concurrently, state and federal programs supporting agriculture and private livestock grazing expanded. Opposition to restoring bison that would compete with livestock, even on our public lands, developed and greatly influenced federal and state law and policy.

Growth of commercial bison herds required state laws to recognize bison as livestock. However, most states failed to recognize bison in their wildlife laws. Bison were left out of 20th century efforts that successfully restored many scarce big game species.

In 2010, the International Union for Conservation of Nature summarized laws regarding bison ownership and management for 20, mostly western, states.[1] In addition, I investigated the legal status of bison in Oregon, Washington and California. All these 23 states have laws recognizing bison as livestock. Only 10 recognize bison as wildlife and IUCN lists "regulatory status" as a major obstacle for bison restoration in 12 of 20 states. Only 4 of the 20 states recognize bison in their recent state comprehensive wildlife plans. Across the USA, most state Natural Heritage Programs have little or nothing to say about native bison. It is as if plains bison never existed. Only

Rewilding Plains Bison

Utah operationally recognizes plains bison as wildlife and had a state plan for bison restoration in 2010. [2]

Aside from Utah, recognition of bison as wildlife by a few states has not resulted in efforts to restore bison. Idaho lists bison as critically imperiled, but has no plan for restoring the species. In Montana, bison are listed as a game species; the state comprehensive wildlife plan refers to establishing free-ranging "disease-free" populations of bison as a possible conservation strategy; and an estimated 70 percent of Montanans support restoration of bison in and around the Charles M. Russell National Wildlife Refuge. However, current Montana law states that it's Fish, Wildlife and Parks Department may not allow wild bison on any land, public or private, where bison have not been authorized to occur. Further, Montana law requires that any restored population of bison must be contained in a pre-designated area, probably with fencing, must be controlled not to exceed "forage carrying capacity", and must remain "disease-free". (Words in quotes are not defined in the state wildlife plan or in state law.) Support of Montanans for restoring wild bison has not yet overcome opposition from the state's livestock industry.

Several states have mostly small, penned herds of bison. From these herds on limited ranges, "excess" bison are auctioned, mostly to commercial bison operators. Public trust bison are converted to private property, a process that is abhorred for other big game species.

No other American big game species has been treated this way. In many states, deer, elk, pronghorn and other species were purposefully brought back from near extinction. Today these species roam freely across the landscape. In many states, private ownership of wildlife, other than bison, is restricted or banned. But for bison, many private bison herds and the first government herds set early examples that free-ranging bison would not be accepted, and that most bison would be managed in captive herds much like cattle. Most state laws sanction domestication of plains bison as livestock.

A notable exception has been the Henry Mountains bison population.

In 1941, Utah obtained bison from Yellowstone National Park and released them in scrub-desert habitat. The animals began using the Henry Mountains as summer range and soon abandoned the lower elevation habitat, remaining year-round in the Mountains. Today, the Henry Mountains bison herd, and the Yellowstone herds are often touted as the only significant free-ranging plains bison herds on native range in the USA. However, while the Henry Mountains herd is unfenced, it is surrounded by unattractive habitat and is, effectively, on a large island.[3]

Recently, Utah released plains bison in the Book Cliffs area under an agreement with the northern Ute tribe which provides some habitat. The future and management of this free-ranging herd will be watched carefully, hopefully as a model for what might be accomplished in other states.

Aside from the lack of public awareness of the plight of wild plains bison, opposition to bison restoration from powerful livestock interests in each state and nationally is the major obstacle to state participation in bison restoration.[4] State livestock organizations have powerful influences upon state legislatures. They tend to exaggerate risks of diseases that may be transmitted from bison to cattle while their major concern is competition for forage, especially for publicly-owned forage on public lands that are used by private livestock (Fig. 10.1).

Along Highway 83, entering Cherry County, Nebraska from the south, a large billboard reads: "Cherry County, God's Own Cow Country." I thought, "Grief! If God has ordained the land for cattle, what chance can there be to restore any wild bison?" The livestock industry promotes itself as a savior of the environment and open spaces. While they find wild bison, and many other wildlife species, unacceptable on lands devoted to cattle; their "good guys" image plays well in all the state capitals.

Although states have vigorously defended their rights to manage wildlife, especially game species, within their borders, state executives and legislators have been reluctant to enter the quagmire of bison politics. They will continue to avoid the issues as long as the public allows. Utah is the only state that embraces wild bison. However, even Utah has ongoing battles with its cattle industry over "too many wild bison."

Fig. 10.1. Stockmen's opposition to bison restoration is intense. On this Montana sign, "federal land grab" refers to a proposal to put public bison on public land – a move that probably would require reducing the number of private livestock on our public land.

Federal Agencies Avoid Bison Controversies

On the surface, policies of federal land management agencies seem to favor restoration of bison on some public lands.[5] The U. S. Forest Service manages National Forests and Grasslands. Its regulations list an objective of "maintaining at least viable populations of all native wildlife in habitats distributed throughout their geographic ranges." The U. S. Fish and Wildlife Service manages our National Wildlife Refuges. The mission of the Refuge system includes conserving a diversity of wildlife and restoring, where appropriate, populations of wildlife and representative ecosystems, including ecological processes. The U. S. Bureau of Land Management oversees extensive lands across the West. Congress declared that these lands be managed on the basis of multiple use, to protect ecological and environmental values, and that some lands be preserved in their natural condition. Multiple use is defined as a combination of uses that considers the long-term needs of future generations for resources, including wildlife. A National Park Service mandate is to leave Park resources, including wildlife, unimpaired for future generations.

Despite these mandates, the federal land management agencies have made little progress toward restoring wild bison. The Bureau of Land Management lacks any clear standards for restoring native species. To my knowledge, the Forest Service has no proposal to restore a viable population of wild bison on its lands. The Park Service and Fish and Wildlife Service have contributed most to bison conservation by maintaining 15 of the 44 conservation herds of plains bison on native range (Chapter 11). However, their efforts toward bison restoration are constrained by the small areas of almost all parks and refuges, and by state restrictions against bison outside these federal lands. All four federal land management agencies have mandates to cooperate or coordinate with laws or policies of surrounding states. As a result, all but 2 of the 15 conservation herds in federal parks or refuges are confined by fences.

With limited space and carrying capacity for bison, the Park Service and the Fish and Wildlife Service must sell or donate "excess" bison. Every year, public trust bison are privatized, or they are donated to Native American reservations where their fate becomes largely unknown.

The Fish and Wildlife Service has refused to review the status of wild bison as possibly threatened or endangered.[6] Among many embarrassments in the Service response to a petition were refusals to recognize the threats of domestication, or loss of genetic diversity, to wild bison. The Service produced the absurdity: "We no longer consider the Yellowstone herd to have remained in a more wild state than any other conservation herd." (See Chapter 11 for a review of plains bison conservation herds. Several conservation herds consist of fewer than 20 penned and fed display animals!)

In late 2011, the Department of Interior suggested to Montana's Governor Schweitzer that restoration of wild bison might begin with new or expanding herds in the Badlands of South Dakota, in a relatively monotonous shrub steppe of the high elevation San Luis Valley of Colorado, or on a Native American reservation in Wyoming. These proposals involve limited, and/or mediocre bison habitat, and bison received by an Indian Nation are no longer public wildlife. These proposals seem to be attempts to assuage growing public concern for the future of wild plains bison with inadequate solutions that create a minimum of controversy.

Essentially, any national interest in bison restoration on large areas of federal land is currently disregarded due to state opposition. Management of our federal lands tends to be subordinated to state and local concerns because our federal legislators, elected within the states, are beholden to state and local self-interests.

For example, the 2010 Draft Conservation Plan for the large Charles M. Russell National Wildlife Refuge states that any proposal to move forward with bison restoration will have to be led by the state of Montana. Are bison not "appropriate", as required in Fish and Wildlife Service regulations, for restoration on the Refuge? It remains to be seen if enough national interest can be generated to force federal leadership and initiative to establish wild bison on any federal lands, let alone on large federal lands with quality bison habitat. Most likely, a critical portion of such national interest must come from densely populated areas in the eastern and western USA. It will require that these populations recognize their majority ownership of federal lands and exercise their will against the current oppositions of minorities within the central states.

Discontinuity of Restoration Effort

Biologists, viewing the political landscape, suggest it may take 100 years of sustained effort to restore wild plains bison widely across the USA.[7] I suspect they are right. However, bison restoration is a highly politicized issue, and most politicians are skeptical of issues that will not be resolved within 2-6 years before the next election. Legislatures and administrations come and go. Planning for restoration of wild bison may begin in one administration and be shelved in the next, leaving some future administration to begin anew. Meanwhile, bison continue to be domesticated.

The most likely and appropriate places for restoring wild bison include large areas with mostly or entirely federal land (Chapter 7). Federal policies tend to be less volatile than those of the states. The melding of public concerns across 50 states provides some stability in federal programs. A sustained effort necessary for restoring wild plains bison on native range in the USA may not occur unless the federal government provides strong, persistent leadership, probably in opposition to some level of state resistance.

However, federal programs are not immune to extreme variation of goals and effort across changes in administrations. For example, the National Park Service commitment, initiated in about 1969, allowing natural processes to dominate in park ecosystems has declined in recent years. Perhaps a reevaluation and recommitment to natural processes within parks will be stimulated by a thorough examination of the issues surrounding wildness of plains bison in the few parks with bison. Retaining wildness is the only way to fulfill the Park Service mandate to leave wildlife "unimpaired for the use and enjoyment of future generations".

The one federal wildlife program that has provided continuity of restoration effort in the face of sometimes strong state opposition has been the Endangered Species Act. Likely, hundreds of species of plants and animals have been saved from oblivion by the ESA. I am convinced that an objective review of the status of wildness in plains bison on native range in the USA would determine that the species qualifies at least as threatened under the ESA. Listing plains bison under the Act may be the only way to initiate and sustain wild plains bison restoration.

Commercial Herds of Plains Bison

More than 90 percent of plains bison, over 220,000 animals in the contiguous USA, are privately owned in over 4,400 commercial herds. Bison ranchers promote their industry through the National Bison Association.[8] The NBA acknowledges unique values of wild bison. Its mission statement includes: "to celebrate the heritage of American bison." NBA alludes to "restoring bison herds across America" and claims that "bison ranching is beneficial to the natural environment."

However, I found nothing in NBA literature that would promote retention of wildness in bison. Bison management is promoted based on the well-tested model for producing and marketing domestic cattle (Fig. 10.2). There are cow-calf operations, grain-finishing programs, a bison registry, bison auctions and bison-judging programs. There are handling instructions for capturing, sorting, testing, treating diseases, loading and confining bison. It is noted that wild bison cows may calve in alternate years whereas, on ranches, bison cows can deliver calves every year, presumably with early, artificial weaning. It is also noted that a bison bull may service 10-15 cows, a prescription to maximize calf production while maintaining a sex ratio that is greatly skewed from ratios of wild herds. Most commercial bison are culled at an early age, once income-producing growth has ceased, but before the full value of fitness is expressed in most animals.

NBA literature cites many characteristics of bison that make them superior to domestic cattle – for management and production of bison products. The fact that commercial bison management will gradually diminish or eliminate these wild characteristics is ignored. Most of the interventions replacing natural selection, listed in Chapter 8, occur in most commercial bison herds. [9]

Several commercial bison ranches augment their incomes by offering bison hunting. A "hunt" may occur in a pasture of 4-5 square miles, or less. However, the ranch manager may drive you to where a bison herd is grazing. A mature bull may be taken for $4000-6000. Bison cows may sell for around $2000. Trophy hunters often prefer 5- or 6

Fig. 10.2. Environments for commercial bison herds vary considerably among operators, sometimes approaching feedlot conditions.

-year old bulls. They have "prettier", unbroomed horns that are more visible because the forelock hair of a younger bull is less dense and shorter than that of an older bull. Harvesting bulls at this young age removes animals before the breeding values of the most fit bulls are realized.

Expansion of commercial bison herds in the USA can indirectly limit restoration of wild plains bison. Wild public bison are a threat to transmit disease to private bison. (It can be argued that commercial bison, more crowded and periodically stressed by handling, are more prone to develop diseases and transmit them to wild bison!) On adjacent habitats, it will probably be difficult to maintain fences between wild and commercial bison, especially during the rut when bulls are apt to challenge fencing. A few commercial bison herds graze in rented allotments on public lands, and there may be more private bison on public lands in the future. This will jeopardize options for restoring wild public bison on our public lands. Given the association of the commercial bison industry with a politically powerful agriculture industry, expansion of commercial bison will be a strong political force against restoring even a few large, wild, public bison herds on public lands in the USA.

Several bison biologists and bison managers have noted: "If bison kept by private ranchers are not included in the ranks of herds that may contribute to ecological recovery, 96% of the world's bison will be lost with one stroke, and an opponent, the bison industry, will have been created where an ally may have stood." [10] However, they do not clarify how the commercial industry may contribute to restoring wild plains bison. The bison industry may not now be a strong opponent of bison restoration, perhaps mostly because there are so few competing bison restoration projects. But the industry has not been a strong supporter of bison restoration. The website of the National Bison Association does not recognize the impacts of its management prescriptions upon wildness in bison and discloses a lack of awareness of the true dimensions of wildness. Even the Fish and Wildlife Service concludes that, "There does not appear to be any conservation value for plains bison in commercial herds." [6]

For restoration of wild plains bison, the expansive views of author and buffalo rancher Dan O'Brien have much to offer.[11] His book, "Buffalo for the Broken Heart" describes much of the limitations, difficulties and opportunities for bison restoration in commercial operations. But O'Brien describes himself as a maverick in a ranching community that resists change. Principle limits to the contributions of the commercial bison industry are the need to make a profit, small, stable herd sizes, lack of public access, and lack of formal long-term commitments, across generations of bison and bison owners, to conserving wildness in bison. Moreover, the abundance of bison in commercial herds can mislead the public into believing that the task of restoring wild bison is finished. Lastly, expansion of the commercial bison industry will diminish opportunities for establishing wild bison populations because it will be difficult to isolate adjacent wild and commercial herds. Today, more than half of our "conservation" herds of plains bison have private, commercial bison herds within 60 miles of their perimeter.[12]

Dale Lott wrote: "To keep bison wild you must be willing to lose money on them – or at least leave money on the table."[13] If the American public learns to understand and wishes to restore the more esoteric values of wild bison, they will have to pay for bison restoration on their own. Delegating the task of bison restoration to commercial producers is an illusion.

Native American Herds of Plains Bison

We owe a debt of gratitude to Walking Coyote of Montana and to the Dupree family of Dakota Territory for their important roles in saving plains bison from numerical extinction.[14] Today, the Intertribal Buffalo Council, with 56 Tribes, is committed to reestablishing bison herds on Indian lands.[15] Member tribes, collectively, manage over 15,000 bison. Largest of these herds are on the Cheyenne River Reservation, South Dakota, with 2000-3000 bison and the Crow Reservation, Montana, with more than 1000. The Intertribal Buffalo Council coordinates education and training programs, develops marketing, coordinates transfer of federal bison to the tribes and provides technical assistance in bison management.

Values of plains bison that are recognized and emphasized by Native Americans vary considerably among individuals and among tribes. Consequently, management of Native American bison herds varies greatly among tribes, and tribal goals and management continue to adapt to evolving attitudes.

Commercial values of tribal bison include the sale of live bison and bison meat, tourism based on bison-viewing, and fee hunting of bison. At least 10 tribes advertise bison hunts. These aspects mirror those of commercial herds managed by non-Indians. Likewise, many tribal bison herds must compete commercially with tribal cattle herds for space, capital investment and management effort on the reservations. The Fort Berthold Reservation recently decreased its bison herd, for commercial reasons, from about 1500 to 130 animals.

Two aspects of tribal bison ownership are unique. Some tribes, especially those of the Great Plains, have deep cultural, spiritual and religious connections to bison. (As a non-Indian, I must use three somewhat redundant adjectives in my attempt to describe a phenomenon that is beyond my roots and understanding.) Also, Native Americans are genetically predisposed to nutritional problems, including diabetes, resulting from much of the modern American diet. An emphasis on low-fat, grass fed bison meat can alleviate this problem. It is especially important on some reservations where poverty and unemployment rates are high.

Commercial motives will not foster a rewilding of plains bison in Indian Country. Some tribal herds are managed much like other commercial bison herds. However, the spiritual connections of Native Americans to bison, especially in some tribes, may lead to some large herds with minimal management on large tracts of diverse habitat. One writer has noted, "Native America remains the bison's best hope for maintaining the wild character of the buffalo." [16] I can only respond, "We shall see what occurs, both within and without Indian Country." In the USA, Native American bison herds have all the problems of our "conservation herds", plus a widespread need for emphasizing commercial and tribal/nutritional values of the animals.

There are opportunities for joint tribal/state management of plains bison herds that may use both tribal and public lands. Perhaps the only example is the new Book Cliffs bison herd in Utah. These few opportunities should be pursued, for they may include large tracts of tribal land where wild bison are welcome to wander. A binding state commitment to a Native American community might offer a rare element in bison conservation – a commitment that lasts across changes in state and tribal politics and leadership.

Religious connections to bison offer the most likely basis for restoring wild bison in Indian Country. However, the concepts of conservation genetics and of evolution and natural selection have little or no part in Native American religions – to my knowledge. As a result, management practices that weaken or replace natural selection are accepted. While we should encourage restoration of bison in Indian Country, on Native American terms, and we should seek new opportunities for joint management of wild bison across reservation boundaries, we should not rely upon Native Americans to restore wild plains bison in the USA. They are moving slowly and they may not succeed. Efforts in Native America do not absolve the rest of us from a responsibility for restoring wild bison.

Private Efforts to Conserve Bison

The Nature Conservancy owns or has an interest in 12 plains bison herds in the contiguous USA. In addition the American Prairie Reserve has plains bison on its holdings in Montana. These herds, designated as livestock in state laws, are included as "conservation herds" that are considered more fully in Chapter 11. Here, I note that only 2 Conservancy herds exceed 500 animals (Medano Ranch, Colorado: 2000 bison; Tallgrass Preserve, Oklahoma: 1950 bison).

Almost all TNC herds are managed much like commercial bison herds, with proceeds from selling bison needed to fund programs of prairie conservation.[17] TNC, to its credit, uses bison grazing to manage and conserve units of native prairie. However, most TNC bison ranges are not large. For this and other reasons, restoration of wild plains bison is not a primary goal for TNC bison herds; with the possible exception of the Medano Ranch herd in Colorado.

In Montana, the American Prairie Reserve is attempting to accumulate a large area of wild prairie with wild plains bison. Restoring wild bison is a primary goal. APR has attempted to obtain pure bison, without cattle genes, and currently has over 200 animals. While these bison are legally classified as domestic livestock by the state of Montana, APR has stated it would donate the animals to

Montana if the opportunity to convert them into public wildlife were to become politically acceptable and legally possible. For purposes of restoring wild plains bison, APR's efforts are especially commendable and exceed most, if not all, public efforts.[18]

Forty-four "Conservation" Herds

The International Union for Conservation of Nature, in its 2010 Status Survey of American Bison,[19] lists 62 "conservation herds" of plains bison in North America. These are herds managed by public agencies and by non-government organizations whose primary mission is nature conservation. Note: the primary mission does not have to be bison conservation. Some conservation herds have very small numbers of animals kept primarily for display, much like animals in a zoo. Still, the focus of restoration for wild plains bison is on these herds, and the U. S. Fish and Wildlife Service contends these 62 herds are sufficient to preclude a review of plains bison status for possible listing as a threatened species. [6]

Here, I contend there are 64 such conservation herds. IUCN does not list the new Tallgrass Prairie National Preserve herd in Kansas and IUCN considers 2 herds at Theodore Roosevelt National Park, North Dakota as one herd. I consider the latter as 2 herds because there is currently no exchange of bison between these herds whose pens are separated by several miles.

Of these 64 plains bison herds, 10 are in Canada and 1 is in Mexico. Nine, in Alaska, California and Arizona, are not on native plains bison range. This leaves 44 conservation herds of plains bison, with about 16,500 animals, on native range in the USA. Of these, 15 are federally owned herds; 15 are state owned; 2 are owned by Denver; 10 are privately owned, mostly by The Nature Conservancy; and 2 have mixed public/private ownership. Characteristics of these 44 herds are reviewed in Chapter 11.

Wildness Denied

The above describes the status of plains bison in the 48 contiguous states as we enter the 21st century. It is clear that the vast majority of the bison genome has been penned under a regime of domestication for over 100 years. Now, a few, mostly small, mostly penned bison herds are promoted, with commercial and Native American herds, as sufficient – for another century of domestication. It is an imitation of wildness and few Americans are aware of the difference. If we do not, as a people, begin to recognize the difference, and recognize the values of truly wild bison, the imitation of wildness will continue as a denial of wild bison for all time. The hope for wild plains bison in the USA currently rests with 44 conservation herds on native range. I rate the conservation value of these 44 herds, for restoring wild bison, in Chapter 11.

Footnotes:

[1] Gates et al. 2010.

[2] Montana conducts numerous operations with bison that enter the state from Yellowstone National Park each winter and spring. These include hunting, hazing, capture and slaughter, vaccination and winter feeding. However, Montana law recognizes these bison primarily as animals in need of disease control, not as wildlife. (See Montana Code 81-2-120 and 87-1-216 as in force during 2012.) The Montana Department of Livestock has much authority over these bison and, as of early 2012, they all must be eliminated or forced back into the Park by May 15 each year.

[3] The Henry Mountains, Utah, bison herd is managed under the 2007 Hunting Unit 15 Management Plan.

[4] At its 2012 convention, the National Cattlemen's Beef Association resolved to oppose relocation of any wild bison outside the current Yellowstone Area or any increase in the current Yellowstone bison

population.

[5] The Forest Service objective is listed in the Forest Service Manual: 2670.21. The mission of the National Wildlife Refuge System is found in the National Wildlife Refuge System Improvement Act of 1997. BLM mandates are in the Federal Land Use Policy and Management Act of 1976. The National Park Service Mandate for leaving resources "unimpaired" is from the 1916 Organic Act establishing the Park Service. The reader is advised that these references are but the tip of the iceberg, above a quagmire of laws, regulations, policies and judicial decisions affecting public and private uses of our public lands.

[6] The Fish and Wildlife Service finding that there is not substantial information warranting a review of plains bison for listing under the Endangered Species Act is in the Federal Register: 76(37)10299-10310, February 24, 2011. The quote regarding lack of conservation value in commercial bison herds is from this document.

[7] The expectation that ecological recovery of plains bison will require another century is cited in Sanderson et al. (2008).

[8] For more on the National Bison Association, see BisonCentral.com.

[9] Callenbach (1996) has described domesticating management in commercial bison herds.

[10] The quote regarding commercial bison herds is from Sanderson et al. (2008).

[11] O'Brien (2002).

[12] Keith Aune, Wildlife Conservation Society, personal communication.

[13] Lott (2002).

[14] Native American contributions to saving plains bison from numerical extinction are described by Zontek (2007). The literature uses both "Dupree" and "Dupuis" as the name of this family.

[15] For the Intertribal Buffalo Council, see itbcbison.com.

[16] J. H. Wood is quoted on p. 92 of Zontek (2007). Considerable Native American concern over the effects of domestication on the wild bison genome is expressed on this page.

[17] Bragg et al. (2002).

[18] For more on the American Prairie Reserve see americanprairie.org.

[19] Gates et al. (2010).

Chapter 11

Rating our Conservation Herds

Today's "Conservation" Herds

As noted in Chapter 10, "conservation herds" of plains bison are those owned by public agencies or by private organizations dedicated to conservation, as defined by the International Union for Conservation of Nature. The 44 conservation herds of plains bison on native range in the USA contain about 16,500 bison. Here, I review some important characteristics of these 44 herds to demonstrate their inadequacy for maintaining wildness in bison. This information comes from personal investigations and from other sources.[1] Characteristics of these herds and their management are dynamic, though changes occur slowly. This review represents conditions during 2010-2011, as best I could discern them.

Herd Size

Thirty-four of our 44 conservation herds of plains bison have 400 or fewer animals (Charts 11.1,11.2). Of these, 19 have 100 or fewer bison. These 34 herds are certainly losing genetic diversity and are in danger of creeping inbreeding, especially the 19 herds with 100 or fewer bison (Chapter 5). Six of these herds are managed, with exchanges of animals among herds, as a federal metapopulation.[2] In addition, a few other conservation herds occasionally exchange breeding bison. This intensive handling of bison may alleviate some inbreeding, but will not eliminate much loss of genetic diversity unless the federal and other herds are greatly expanded. Herds with fewer than 2000 - 3000 bison have compromised evolutionary potentials (Chapter 5). There are only 4 conservation herds south of Canada with more than 1000 bison, and only the Yellowstone National Park herd is large enough to limit loss of genetic diversity to moderate levels in the long term.

Chart 11.1. Conservation herds of plains bison on native USA range, 2011.

	Number of bison	Range (sq. mi.)
* Yellowstone NP, WY, MT	3700	3500
* Medano Ranch, TNC, CO	2000	70
* Tallgrass Preserve, TNC, OK	1950	36
* Custer SP, SD	1100	110
* Wichita Mtns. NWR, OK	650	67
* Badlands NP, SD	600	100
* Ft. Robinson, SP, NE	500	5
* Niobrara Valley, TNC, NE	500	30
* Antelope Island, UT	500	43
* Jackson Valley, WY	500	110
* Wind Cave NP, SD	400	43
* National Bison Range, MT	350	29
* T. Roosevelt NP South, ND	350	72
Clymer, TNC, TX	320	2
* Ordway Prairie, TNC, SD	300	5
** Henry Mtns., UT	300	45
* Ft. Niobrara NWR, NE	290	25
* Konza Prairie, KS	275	4
Broken Kettle, TNC, IA	250	4
* Cross Ranch, TNC, ND	200	6
* Amer. Prairie Reserve, MT	200	50
* T. Roosevelt NP North, ND	175	38
* Maxwell State Reserve, KS	165	4
Land between Lakes, KY	120	1
** Prairie SP, MO	120	5
* Tallgrass Nat. Preserve, KS	100	2
Book Cliffs, UT	100	uncertain
Neal Smith NWR, IA	71	3
* Caprock SP, TX	62	1
* Sully at Ft. Niobrara NWR, NE	61	shared
Blue Mounds SP, MN	56	1

Chart 11.1 continued

** Rocky Mtn. Arsenal, CO	55	4
Smoky Valley, TNC, KS	45	5
** Genesee Park, CO	34	1
Fermi Lab, IL	32	<0.5
** Daniels Park, CO	28	1
* Sandsage State Preserve, KS	20	6
Sandhill State Wildl. Area, WI	15	<0.5
Hot Springs SP, WY	11	1
Bear Butte SP, SD	11	?
Wildcat Hills State Recr. Area, NE	10	1
Bear River SP, WY	8	<0.5
Sully's Hill NWR, ND	7	1
Lame Johnny Creek, TNC, SD	?	for sale
Total bison	16,541	

* 24 herds visited in this study. ** 5 herds, managers contacted by mail in this study. SP = State Park. NWR = National Wildlife Refuge. TNC = The Nature Conservancy.

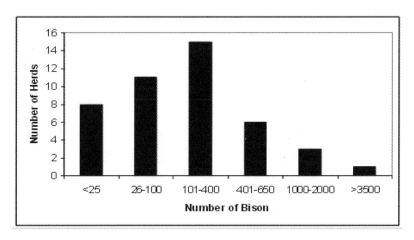

Chart 11.2. Sizes of 44 conservation herds of plains bison on native range in the USA, 2011.

Aside from maintaining genetic diversity, large bison herds allow evolved social/dominance relations to contribute normally to natural selection. Almost all our conservation herds are maintained with low, relatively stable numbers of bison living at relatively low ecological densities. This weakens natural selection for wild traits that adapt bison to living in both good and bad times (Chapter 5).

Range Size

At least 11 of the 44 conservation herds of plains bison on native range in the USA live on ranges of no more than a square mile (Charts 11.1,11.3). These are only display herds in exhibition pens. Their contribution to the future of wild bison will be minimal, at best. More than 60% of the 44 conservation herds have ranges of 10 or fewer square miles.

Only 4 of the 44 herds have ranges of at least 100 square miles (Charts 11.1,11.3). However, 3 of these come with limitations for wild bison: (1) Bison range at Badlands National Park includes much

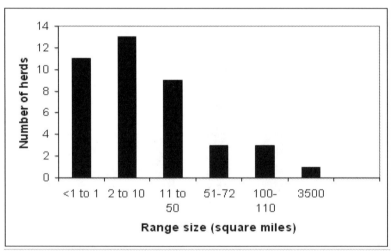

Chart 11.3. Range sizes for 44 conservation herds of plains bison on native range in the USA, 2011.

barren ground. (2) Most of the 110 square miles within Custer State Park is forested. There are but 28 square miles of grassland to provide optimal bison habitat. (3) The Jackson Valley, Wyoming bison herd, with about 110 square miles of available range, will be limited to 500 animals and is artificially fed during winter. Even the Yellowstone National Park herd of plains bison, which roams over about 3500 square miles, has important limitations. Their range is mostly high elevation habitat. Bison leaving this range during severe winters or seeking early-spring green forage have been culled or penned and fed. An interagency team including the state of Montana is seeking to find additional range where Yellowstone bison will be welcome.

Obviously, small ranges limit the numbers of bison that can be sustained. Moreover, a large, diverse habitat is necessary for bison to express many of their ecological relations with the environment (Chapter 3). Bison evolved as mobile grazers selecting forage patches and habitats as needed to meet changing vegetation and weather conditions. These abilities lose their value and will not be maintained by natural selection when bison are tightly confined.

The small range sizes for almost all these 44 conservation herds of plains bison are a major limitation for wildness and a major factor leading to domestication of the species.

Interior Fencing

Ranges of at least 14 conservation herds are subdivided by cross-fencing so that bison may be periodically rotated among pastures. This constrains bison from selecting foraging habitat and creates unnatural foraging effects upon vegetation. Rest-rotation grazing is necessary to support more than a very few bison on several small bison ranges. However, at least 8 herds with more than 100 bison are managed with rotation grazing systems, much like domestic livestock. This reflects a prevalent thinking of bison as livestock, and a common need to produce large numbers of bison for sale, with proceeds often used to fund continuing intensive management of bison.

Roundups and Handling

At least 25 of the 44 conservation herds are subjected to annual, or more frequent, roundups and handling by running animals through pens and handling chutes. At least 8 more herds have less frequent, but regular roundups with handling. These roundups facilitate many of the practices leading to domestication of bison (Chapter 8).

Selective Culling

Selective culling of bison to control herd size is routine in 35 of the 44 conservation herds, and probably will occur in 5 more herds when their bison numbers reach established goals. As bison are removed periodically from these 40 herds, few bison managers emphasize randomness in selecting animals for removal or retention. Animals are removed based on sex, age, size, appearance and behavior. Sometimes selection is an unconscious process. Inadvertent selection for characteristics based on genetically-linked traits likely is common. In this manner, selective culling is a major factor weakening or replacing natural selection (Chapter 8).

Often, culling is used to remove bison by middle age. Older bulls become difficult to handle. Older bison are no longer growing, producing meat; and they are less valuable for sale. However, bison are removed from the herds before the full values of the fittest individuals are fully realized in natural selection.

Numbers of bison are or will be managed primarily with hunting in only 3 herds in Utah and Wyoming. Selection of animals for harvest is influenced by hunter choice and by hunting rules. Hunting rules are rarely, if ever, based upon any consideration of evolutionary effects. These effects of hunting are uncertain and will depend largely upon the proportion of natural mortality that is replaced with harvest. Lastly, the Yellowstone Park bison herd is limited by a combination of significant natural mortality, hunting outside the Park, and selective culling of animals with roundups. Bison carrying antibodies against *Brucella* infection are emphasized in this culling, although some culled animals are not infected and some may be the most *Brucella*-resistant individuals.

Rating our Conservation Herds

Natural Mortality

Of 28 conservation herds that I contacted during 2010-2011, it was noted that "very few" bison die naturally on the range in 18 of the herds. Herd sizes are controlled by regular removals of animals. Significant natural mortality was noted in only 6 of these 28 herds. The remaining 4 herds were new or had a new management plan, such that the amount of natural mortality that will occur has not been tested. While these numbers relate to 28 of the 44 conservation herds, it is likely that natural mortality is even less common in the 16, mostly smaller, herds I did not contact. The percentage of conservation herds without significant natural mortality is almost certainly much larger than indicated by my survey.

Supplemental Feeding

Thirteen of our 44 conservation herds of plains bison are routinely fed, at least seasonally. However, at least 8 other herds are fed during "crisis" periods of forage deprivation, usually during periods with deep snow, occasionally during drought. So, for at least 21 of 44 conservation herds, natural selection for dominant, energy efficient bison (Chapter 4) is at least weakened. In addition, unnatural concentrations of bison in feeding areas results in unnaturally increased rates of disease transmission among animals, and increased densities of disease organisms in the feedground environment.

Disease Management

At least 17 of our 44 conservation herds of plains bison are regularly vaccinated for from 1 to 8 diseases. In addition, vermicides to control internal and external parasites are applied in many of these 17 herds. These practices weaken natural selection for disease resistant bison and modify coevolution of disease organisms (Chapters 4, 8). Unintended effects may involve resistance to and evolution of disease species other than those targeted by each specific vaccine.

Active vermicides, passing through a bison's digestive tract, may act as insecticides in bison feces. Effects on the flora and fauna of bison feces, and on rates of nutrient turnover in the environment have not been studied.

Bull:Cow Ratios

At least 16 of our 44 conservation herds are managed with skewed, or highly skewed, adult bull:cow ratios of 1:3 to 1:15. This weakens or eliminates the important natural-selective value of bull competition (Chapter 5). It is encouraging that at least 20 of the 44 herds are managed with more natural adult bull:cow ratios near 1:1. Some management agencies, especially the National Park Service and the U. S. Fish and Wildlife Service, recognize the natural-selective values of bull competition.

Predators

Of the 44 conservation herds, only the Yellowstone Park herd faces significant natural predation by bears and wolves. Bison also live with these predators in Jackson Valley, Wyoming. However, there has been very little predation on bison in this area where numerous elk on winter feedgrounds are the primary prey. It seems unlikely that the significant natural-selective values of predation will be restored in any other conservation herds in the near future.

Legal Status

At least 28 of the 44 conservation herds are located in states, or parts of states, where bison have no legal recognition as wildlife. These state laws recognize bison only as livestock (Chapter 10).

Synopsis

Summarizing the above for the 44 plains bison conservation herds on native range in the USA:

- Herds with fewer than 400 bison   77%
- Ranges 10 or less square miles   >60%
- Rest/rotation grazing management   32%, at least
- Roundups and handling   >75%

Rating our Conservation Herds

- Selective culling   >80%
- Little or no natural mortality   >64%
- Supplemental feeding   48%, at least
- Vaccinations, etc.   39%
- Skewed bull:cow ratio   36%
- No effective predators   95%
- No state legal status as wildlife   >64%.

Wild Bison Scorecard

The above review of domesticating practices in our 44 conservation herds of plains bison on native range in the USA causes much concern for the future of the species. While alarming, this review could be misleading if herd limitations and artificial management that diminish wildness are concentrated in a subset of the 44 herds, while another subset remains relatively wild. In contrast, every herd may have some significant problems, with few or no really wild herds. To assess this possibility, I needed to rate and combine values for several wildness characteristics, producing an average "wildness score" for each herd.

In 2008, a convention of 28 bison biologists published a "scorecard" for measuring contributions of bison herds to ecological recovery of the species.[3] The complex scorecard provides 5 standards of ecological recovery for each of 18 rating factors: a large 18 X 5 matrix. The authors considered their scorecard as a work in progress, needing refinement to become operational. Still, it is an excellent summary of the issues and requirements for restoring wild bison. It should influence those who manage bison with a goal of restoring and maintaining wildness.

However, I need a simple scorecard to communicate the status of wildness in plains bison today. With apologies to those 28 biologists, I have selectively abstracted their contribution into a much simpler matrix (Chart 11.4). One may argue I have oversimplified: that I have not selected the 12 most important wildness categories; or that I have omitted important herd characteristics related to the future of wildness in plains bison. I admit there are such issues; but suggest that, for all the tweaking that might be done with my simple scorecard, results would be quite similar anyway. I choose not to wait for a consensus on the relative importance of every factor related to wildness in plains bison. Consensus may never come.

I rated each of 12 factors of wildness at 4 levels along the domestic-to-wild continuum (Chart 11.4). My somewhat arbitrary selection and scoring of factors is based on the foregoing chapters. I include "public access" as a scoring factor although it is not likely to have a significant impact on natural selection and the genetics of wildness in bison. I include public access because there will be less value in retaining wild bison if few people can visit, view, enjoy and use their wild bison herd.

I used the scorecard to assess the values of 28 herds for restoring and maintaining wildness in plains bison in the USA. These herds are noted with asterisks in Chart 11.1. For this analysis, I combined 2 herds, the Fort Niobrara National Wildlife Refuge herd and the herd from Sully's Hill Preserve, now at Fort Niobrara NWR. These herds have the same management regime.

The 28 analyzed herds include the 13 largest conservation herds and 23 of the 27 conservation herds with at least 100 bison. The observed herd characteristics and management practices I scored for these herds can change over a few to several years. In two cases, I credited conservation herds with more or fewer bison than existed during my investigation, using the stated management goals for animal numbers when one herd was being allowed to grow and another was being reduced. However, I believe my results present a fair picture of the wildness vs. domestication status of 28 of the most important conservation herds during 2010-2011.

My subset of 28 of the 44 conservation herds of plains bison on native range in the USA is, no doubt, biased towards the wildest herds, because I selected mostly the largest among the 44 conservation herds. The average herd size for the 28 scored herds is 553 bison (range = 20 – 3700). The average herd size for 15 of the 16 unscored herds is 70 bison (range = 7 – 320. (One small herd is omitted.). Results from this subset of 28 scored herds understate the prevalence of domestication in our 44 conservation herds because elements of domestication are more common in the smaller herds.

In scoring these herds during 2010-2011, I visited 23 herds to discuss management practices with bison managers. I also contacted 5 bison managers by phone or e-mail. I choose not to identify most herds in this discussion because comparisons among closely ranked herds are not justified. Neither methods nor results are sufficiently precise for such comparisons.

Maximum wildness on my scorecard would result in a score of 36 points. I arbitrarily classify scores as: 0-9, domestic; 10-17, semidomestic; 18-27, semiwild; and 28-36, wild. (These arbitrary definitions, simply quartering 36, are used only to facilitate describing the results.)

Wildness Values of "Conservation" Herds

Ordinating the wildness scores (Chart 11.5) shows a continuous trend from domestic to wild herds. One state herd, with 5 points, stands out as being exceptionally domesticated (Fig. 11.1). Only two herds met my arbitrary criterion of wild. The overall average score was 17.6, right on the cusp between semi-domestic and semi-wild. About half the herd scores exceeded this benchmark of mediocre wildness.

Chart 11.4. WILDNESS CHARACTERISTICS OF PLAINS BISON HERDS
A Brief Scorecard

Wildness Score	Domestic 0	Semi-Domestic 1	Semi-Wild 2	Wild 3
1. Herd Size*	<100	100-500	500-200	>2000
2. Range	<3 sq. mi.	3-10 sq. mi.	10-500 sq. mi.	>500 sq. mi.
3. Constriction	Tightly confined	Exterior and interior fences	Exterior fences only	Fences only in conflict Areas
4. Roundups	Annual	Biennial	Occasional	None
5. Population control**	Stable herd (<$\leq$* 10%)	Little natural fluctuation (10-25%)	Modest natural fluctuation (>25%)	Unregulated
6. Culling***	Highly selective by sex & age, commercial purposes	Some selection for commercial purposes. Very few die on the range	Random culling, juveniles only. Most adults die on the range	Hunting only, on the range
7. Disease control	Annual, several diseases	Routine, $\geq$1 diseases	Rarely	Never

Rating our Conservation Herds

Chart 11.4. continued

8. Feeding	Constant	Seasonal	In crisis only	Never
9. Public access	None	Perimeter only	<50% of area, time open	Few or no restrictions
10. Cattle genes	>5% of markers show introgression	<2-5% of markers show introgression	<2% of markers show introgression	No known introgression
11. State legal status	Livestock only, wild bison prohibited	State has legal constraints for wild bison	Bison are wildlife in state recovery plan	Bison are wildlife in state recovery goals
12. Ecological interactions	Few native vertebrates, artificial habitat	10-50% of native vertebrates, >20% artificial habitat	Most native verebrates, >80% natural habitat	Complete, natural ecosystem****

* Breeding herd size, usually measured over-winter or post-culling.
** Population control limits the amount of natural variation in herd size. So for "Modest Fluctuation", the herd would be artificially manipulated or culled whenever it deviated by 25% from its long-term average herd size.
*** Culling for commercial purposes includes managing the sex- and age-structure of the population, and/or culling to select for body conformations.
**** Complete natural ecosystem = essentially all native vertebrates present, including at least one effective bison predator species.

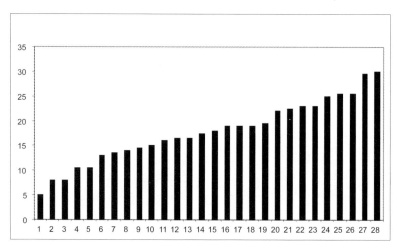

Chart 11.5. Wildness values for 28 of the 44 plains bison conservation herds on native range in the USA. See text for explanation of wildness scoring.

Fig. 11.1. Bison feeders in display pen at Caprock State Park, TX. Artificial watering facilities are nearby. Note paucity of natural forage for bison.

Rating our Conservation Herds

For each of the 12 wildness factors, a herd may be rated from 0 to 3. (In some cases, I awarded half points for intermediate situations.) The overall average score per factor was 1.46, which is low but not very interesting. However, average scores (across herds) for each of the wildness factors are of interest. They may demonstrate pervasive problems throughout our conservation herds of plains bison. These average factor-scores are:

- State legal status of bison   0.46
- Roundups and handling   0.70
- Managed herd stability   0.79
- Herd size   1.15
- Culling practices   1.41
- Range size   1.44
- Cattle-gene introgression   1.67
- Interior range fencing   1.69
- Disease management   1.79
- Ecological relations   2.04
- Public access   2.19
- Supplemental feeding   2.20

Thus, the most pervasive wildness deficiencies in conservation herds of plains bison in the USA are the first three cited above.

The confusing and lacking legal status of wild plains bison was cited by the International Union for Conservation of Nature as "the single most important obstacle impeding ecological restoration and hindering a nationwide conservation strategy".[4] My low average score for state legal status, above, coincides with this conclusion.

Rewilding Plains Bison

In this subset of conservation herds, the 2nd most pervasive problem for conserving wildness in plains bison is the prevalence of roundups and bison handling. Only 8 of the 28 herds are rounded up less than annually or not at all.

Almost equally pervasive is the prevalent practice of controlling bison numbers to maintain stable herd sizes at relatively low ecological densities. In a review of the bison conservation literature, I found the subverting impact upon natural selection from maintaining a stable, relatively low population of bison is not recognized.

At the other extreme, any lack of natural ecological relations, public access, and use of supplemental feeding were the 3 least prevalent problems for wildness in my subset of 28 evaluated conservation herds.

While most of these herds are in relatively natural environments, only 2 live with effective predators. A high score for public access provides little comfort because, unlike the other 11 factors, public access will have little direct impact upon the genetics of wildness in bison. The high score for supplemental feeding misrepresents the prevalence of this practice across all 44 conservation herds. I expect supplemental feeding is more common in the smaller conservation herds living on smaller bison ranges, whereas my sample emphasized the largest herds.

Overall, my analysis of 28 of the wildest herds confirms and accentuates conclusions reached in the above review of all 44 conservation herds. Practices leading to domestication are common throughout these herds, and very common in most of them. There is no subset of conservation herds that scores well for most or all the wildness criteria.

In this subset emphasizing the wildest of the 44 plains bison conservation herds on native range in the USA, a strong majority of herds is rated as either semi-domestic or semi-wild (Chart 11.5). Most of the wildest herds are located in the northern Great Plains and the Rocky Mountains. All but one of several herds in the central Great Plains is rated semi-domestic. Most of the wildest herds are managed

194

by the National Park Service and the US Fish and Wildlife Service. A majority of the most-domesticating herds are managed by the states, local governments and private organizations.

Our "Wildest" Plains Bison Herds

Based on the above criteria, the two wildest plains bison herds on native range in the USA are in the Henry Mountains of Utah and in the Yellowstone Park area. But how wild are these herds? Each has severe limitations detracting from their value as our best examples of wild plains bison to leave for future generations.

Aside from living in an unusual bison habitat surrounded by semi-desert shrubland, the Henry Mountains herd is limited to 325 animals. This low number fosters some degree of inbreeding and is far below the number of bison needed to thwart genetic drift and maintain genetic diversity. As of 2011, Utah has not addressed the inbreeding issue. Periodically bringing additional genes from another herd into the Henry Mountains herd should be considered. The Henry Mountains bison originated from Yellowstone Park and appear to be free of cattle-gene introgression. Maintaining this genetic purity is desirable. Therefore, Utah should consider obtaining bison from the Yellowstone herd or from one of the few herds that originated with Yellowstone bison and has remained cattle-gene free. Still, periodic interjection of "new blood" into the Henry Mountains bison herd will do little to combat losses due to genetic drift in this small herd.

Yellowstone National Park has our premier herd of wild plains bison. Yellowstone is the only place where wild bison were not eliminated about 100 years ago. All other herds have been reestablished with bison from captive herds. While a few captive bison from Texas and Montana were once added to the Yellowstone herd, there has, as yet, been no evidence of cattle-gene introgression. However, the Park bison are infected with *Brucella abortus* and live among a large population of *Brucella*-infected elk.

Despite the low and controllable risk of bison infecting domestic livestock with brucellosis, the Park Service and Montana have subjected Yellowstone bison to several interventions that replace or weaken natural selection and lead toward domestication. Herd size has been limited with selective culling. Bison have been vaccinated. In the winter of 2011, up to 700 bison were held and fed for up to 4 months in crowded pens (Figs. 8.5, 11.2). Bison that leave the Park in early spring are driven back into the Park each May (Fig. 11.3). Additional domesticating interventions are being considered, including an additional pen for holding and feeding more bison in winter and an attempt to remotely vaccinate all Park bison, including very many that never leave the Park and pose no risk to livestock. Experiments with immuno-contraceptive drugs are being conducted. Even our most wild herd of plains bison on native range in the USA is being subjected to many interventions that jeopardize its wild genome.

Fig. 11.2 Facilities for handling "wild" bison inside Yellowstone National Park.

Fig. 11.3. Bison leaving Yellowstone National Park to have their calves amid fresh green forage at lower elevations are rounded up and driven back into the Park each May (Buffalo Field Campaign photo).

Pervasive Domestication of Plains Bison

This summary of the wildness status of 44 conservation herds of plains bison, and the more intensive analysis of a subset of 28 of these herds, demonstrate pervasive, ongoing domestication of the plains bison genome. This insidious threat is more serious than cattle-gene introgression. It is more serious than the loss of genetic diversity because gradual domestication is receiving less attention (and loss of genetic diversity is part of the domestication process). The brush with extinction is not over. For more than 100 years, we have been slowly domesticating plains bison, leading to genetic extinction of the wild form.

Footnotes

[1] During 2010-2011, I Surveyed 28 of the largest and most important conservation herds of plains bison on native range in the USA. This information was supplemented with data from Boyd (2003) and from Dratch and Gogan (2010).

[2] Jones and Roffe (2008) recommended this USFWS metapopulation

strategy. Its implementation is described in Refuge Update, USFWS, January/February, 2011.

[3] Sanderson et al. (2008).

[4] Gates et al. (2010).

Part IV

Restoration of Wild Plains Bison

In wilderness is the preservation of the wild bison genome.
(with acknowledgment to Henry David Thoreau)

The path toward restoring wild bison is not entirely clear.
Much remains to be tested and learned.

However, if we wait for all the answers, we will never restore wild
bison. We must go to learn, and learn as we go.

Chapter 12
To Restore Wild Plains Bison

We are committed to domesticating most of our plains bison. The process is well under way in over 4000 private commercial bison herds in every state. The threat of domestication to the minority of bison in our conservation herds has been exposed in the foregoing chapters. Throughout, I have alluded to perceptions and management practices necessary for restoring wild plains bison in the USA. At the risk of more redundancy, I juxtapose these ideas here. This is necessary to deal with the number and interrelatedness of the issues. The path toward restoring wild bison is not entirely clear. Much remains to be tested and learned as we move forward. I offer these ideas only as a start in the direction of restoring wild plains bison.

Evolution of Wildlife Conservation

Bison restoration has been a lagging component in the development of wildlife conservation in America. In the past 100 years, the thought, science and practice of wildlife conservation have expanded and evolved. Along the way, game management became wildlife management, and now wildlife conservation – a broader endeavor that includes more than just game production and hands-on management.

In the beginnings of game management, the emphasis was almost solely on numbers of animals. In the late 19th century, there were concerns over scarce numbers of game, "excess" numbers of predators, and continued depletion of game "stocks" toward near- or complete-extermination by commercial harvesting and poaching. (The term "stock" is seldom applied to wildlife today, having its roots with domestic livestock management.)

Early efforts at game management focused on these problems of animal numbers. First, there were laws to prohibit or regulate harvest of animals. This was soon followed by indiscriminate predator control, artificial propagation and releasing of game, and translocating animals from remaining populations into areas of extirpation. All these tools of wildlife management remain in use today, usually in modified or limited applications.

As time passed, there was an increasing awareness that saving animals was of no avail unless we also saved and restored habitats where wildlife could live and prosper. Theodore Roosevelt and the early Boone and Crockett Club were promoters of wildlife reserves, refuges and national parks. Unfortunately, many reserve boundaries were based on factors other than the year-round needs of migratory large mammals. Often, harvest was not allowed in these areas. Increasing game stocks were expected to expand and repopulate surrounding lands off the reserves. A growing science of ecology soon began to provide additional awareness of the complex and intricate relations between wild animals and their habitats. Providing quality habitat, as best we could define it, largely through manipulation of the vegetation, became a basic wildlife management tool. This was the "most-evolved" stage of game management alluded to by Aldo Leopold in 1933.[1]

Continued evolution of thought and practice in wildlife conservation has emphasized, not just numbers of animals and acres of habitat, but the qualities of these resources. In particular, modern advances in genetics have elevated concerns for genetic diversities and evolutionary potentials of wildlife populations. On the habitat side, ecological science has begun to demonstrate the enormous complexity of the biota and its relations to soils and hydrology, that is, the complexity of ecosystems. This has fostered some humility among those who predict and develop schemes for managing wildlife and habitats. (As usual, Aldo Leopold pointed this way in his "Round River" essay, published in 1953.)

In this evolution of wildlife conservation, there has been a gradually increasing focus, not on single components of ecosystems such as game or endangered species populations, but on values of complete wild ecosystems. In the increasingly populated and developed United States, wildness continues to dwindle and the values of our few wild places grow with their increasing rarity.

To Restore Wild Plains Bison

The rescue and restoration of plains bison have reflected this evolution in wildlife conservation. Earliest efforts were to save a few animals and to end commercial and illegal harvest. Provision of habitat for captive herds of bison began at Wichita Mountains, Oklahoma in 1907. Today, much of the focus of plains bison management in the USA is on restoring and maintaining the genetic qualities of conservation herds and on restoring the ecological role of plains bison in a few small-to-moderate sized grassland ecosystems. Indeed, in the 2008 guiding statement for restoring North American bison, effects of bison on grasslands were emphasized.[2] However, I believe the reciprocal effects of wild grassland ecosystems on wildness of bison were insufficiently explored. This deficiency has been noted in the 2010 Status Survey of American Bison in which the threats of creeping domestication are recognized.[3] But discussion of the issue has barely begun and public awareness of the issue is minimal. Bison conservation evolves slowly, but the current and challenging bison issues may now lead thought and practice in the larger field of wildlife conservation.

Wildness as a Goal

There has been little articulation of wildness as a goal for the future of plains bison. The mostly recent endorsement of a prevalence of natural selection as the criterion of wildness rests on simple premises:

- Wild bison evolved in a wild past, but evolution has not ceased.

- In small and captive herds, few founders, cattle-gene introgression, inbreeding, genetic drift and artificial selection weaken or replace natural selection and diminish wild characteristics of bison.

- We don't leave bison to future generations of Americans. We leave the bison genome. Therefore, if we are to leave any wild bison to future generations, we must provide a substantial number of bison in some large, wild habitats where natural selective forces predominate to determine and maintain the wild bison genome.

Rewilding Plains Bison

We will not restore wild plains bison without widespread public support for dedicating some public land to bison and to diverse wild grasslands. But, current public understanding of the meaning, dimensions and needs of wildness is lacking. We have been warehousing bison in pens for so long that we have forgotten what wildness means. Many Americans have an idyllic view of wildness and wilderness. They perceive wildness in the context of a perfect balance of nature. This perception is far from true. The "balance" of nature is dynamic. Variation among good and lean periods can be great. Wet times follow droughts. Severe winters and epidemics of disease occur. Wild populations may respond with wide fluctuations in abundance.

Moreover, nature can be brutal. Animals starve and they die in the cold. Many young and the old are killed by predators. Diseases take their toll or increase the risk of predation. Competition among males causes injuries, even death; and may relegate some males to life without reproducing. This is the process of wildness. It is the process of natural selection maintaining only those animals and those genetic combinations best suited for living and reproducing in the wild. It keeps wildlife alert, efficient, mobile, agile, strong, enduring and disease-resistant. We may not remove the harshness without destroying the wildness.

In today's wildlife management, there are very many combinations of management practices along the domestic-to-wild continuum (Chart 12.1). Many big game populations are only semi-wild, if not semi-domestic. Truly wild big game are quite rare in the USA outside of Alaska. To retain the "wild" in wildlife, we should manage some big game populations to be as wild as possible and practical. The issue of preserving wildness in bison may force us to face this issue with other big game species.

Chart 12.1. The domestic-wild continuum in big-game management, collapsed into three columns and simplified. The domestic and wild extremes are well defined, whereas the center with semi-wild animals is broad and highly variable.

	Domestic Animals	Semi-Wild Animals	Wild Animals
Example	Game ranching	Wildlife management	National Park, Reserve
Mission	Economic	Modified production	Unimpared naturalness
Interventions	Intensive	Varys, few to many	Restrained
Populations	Stable	Dampened fluctuations	Fluctuating
Movements	Controlled	Limited or managed	Unrestrained
Aggregations	Often large	Sometimes managed	Due to natural behavior
Habitat diversity	Much limited	Managed	Natural diversity

Chart 12.1. continued

Natural mortality	Unacceptable	Limited	Evolutionary process
Predators	Controlled or eliminated	Modified, perhaps greatly	Valued
Diseases	Controlled or eliminated	Sometimes managed	Evolving resistance, accomodation
Artificial food, water	Routine	Sometimes provided	Not provided
Population age structure	Young	Modified	Varys, often old
Population sex ratio	Mostly female	Often modified	Natural, often even
Genetic selection Genetic diversity	Artificial Usually ignored	Compromised natural Often ignored	Natural Valued
Major values	Maximum sustained income	Recreational with commercial aspects	Rarity, Scientific, Esthetic
In USA, outside AK	Common	Declining	Very rare

To Restore Wild Plains Bison

Free-ranging Bison

The possibility for a wild bison herd that wanders over thousands of square miles is unlikely. Outside of Nevada, our country is too dissected by property boundaries, fences, and interstate highways. Land east of about 98 degrees west longitude is especially fully developed. It is in the central and western portions of the USA where wild plains bison may be restored. Large grassland reserves with bison are possibilities in the western Great Plains and in the greater Yellowstone Area. A very large reserve, but with mediocre bison habitat, is possible in Nevada or Oregon.

If we are to have wild plains bison there must be more emphasis on fencing bison out of places where they are not welcome; and less emphasis on fencing bison in. Ultimately, where the fencing out option is abundant, the line between fencing out and fencing in becomes blurred.

Purists will prefer no fences in the management of wild bison – that bison should roam as freely as do deer, elk and other wildlife. But bison are different. They are our largest terrestrial mammal, and they may come by the hundreds. One herd may destroy a wheat field in a day. Our country is too full and developed for a totally unrestricted bison herd. Fences and other means for controlling bison distribution will be necessary where there are real and demonstrated issues for private property or public safety.

The possibility of using herding and hazing to train a newly established bison herd to use desired migration corridors and seasonal habitats should be explored.

If bison are fenced or otherwise limited to a range that is large enough, we might justify that they are "free-ranging". But how large a range is needed to solve this semantic problem? It's stuff for eternal discussion that will not move restoration of wild plains bison forward. The sizes of wild bison ranges will be determined by political realities, not by semantic arguments, nor even by biology. I suggest 100 square miles as an arbitrary minimum area for wild free-ranging bison; but promote 500 square miles of diverse habitat as a goal for at least a few bison ranges. Five-hundred square miles could provide bison with many options for exploiting their environment and would allow a diversity of natural selection to operate. Moreover, hunting bison on an area of this size would be "fair-chase" hunting, not just harvesting bison in a large pen.

How large is 500 square miles? If it is a square, it is only 22.4 miles on a side.

In the West, many blocks of public land are at least this large, though some would be suboptimal bison habitat because the public lands are largely those left over after the best lands were successfully privatized.

We should find a few places with large amounts of mostly contiguous public land where there is a possibility for assembling at least 500 square miles of mostly public bison range. We should state our public intention to achieve this goal as opportunities arise, including land traded or purchased from willing sellers. If we do not take this approach, we will never really get started. Once established, bison could be allowed to roam over this landscape, just like deer, pronghorn, or other public wildlife. Clear obstacles, such as a major highway where bison would be hazardous, could be fenced, ideally with underpasses that allow safe wildlife passage. Wherever bison roam without welcome on private land, they might be fenced out. Where public lands give way to mostly private lands, and bison are unwelcome, we will have to fence bison in. However, we should compare the efficacy and efficiency of fencing to limit bison distribution vs. timely and geographically targeted public hunting, strategic hazing, and - if necessary - capture and relocation or slaughter by public agents. But the goal of at least 500 square miles without internal barriers should be accepted as a realistic long-term possibility at the beginning of restoration.

Other areas, where 500 square miles of bison habitat is not currently a realistic goal, should not be neglected. The same process and commitment, described above, could be used to establish some bison ranges of 100-500 square miles. However, it is probably not worthwhile to use resources, or political capital, to promote bison ranges of less than 100 square miles. We have enough small plains bison ranges with penned herds where bison are being domesticated (Chapter 11).

There will be a tendency for government administrators to draw a line on a map to buy politically-charged acceptance of a grassland reserve with a commitment to limiting, for all time, the size and location of the reserve. A line on a map is acceptable, but a commitment to never modify the line is unworkable and unwise. Our knowledge of bison genetics is incomplete. Will 2000-3000 bison always be considered a satisfactory number to maintain genetic integrity of a herd? Likewise, our knowledge of bison ecology is incomplete, particularly for bison in the Rocky Mountains and Far West. We cannot predict how bison will use the landscape to maintain all their natural responses to varying challenges and opportunities of their environment. However, given the chance and a diverse habitat to explore, bison will show us what they need. Future decisions to modify an established bison range should be based upon the best available knowledge of the time.

Fences

Those opposed to restoring wild plains bison have contended that extreme fences are needed to retain bison, and that even these fences will routinely fail. Yet bison are contained with modest fencing in more than 4,000 commercial herds and in most conservation herds (Figs. 12.1, 12.2, 12.3). Fencing needs will vary with site conditions, both among and within bison ranges. Fencing needs will also vary with the amount and diversity of habitat available within the fence, and as bison learn and establish movement patterns within the fenced area. Challenges to fences may not always be predicted before a new bison herd is established. Existing herds indicate that effective bison fencing can be developed with experience and that elaborate fences are not needed in most places.

Fig. 12.1 Many fences used to contain bison herds are quite modest, such as this 5-strand barbed wire . . . .

.....however, most bison managers use tall fences, such as this 7-strand fence.

Fig. 12.2 This 7-foot fence keeps bison from an interstate highway in North Dakota.

Fig. 12.3 In bison country, barriers at road crossings are usually more elaborate, and often longer than this or the standard "cattle guards". But this guard has been effective in bison country.

How Many Bison?

Too often, controversial restoration of wildlife has descended into the minimalist/defensive mode of determining the smallest number of animals that might assure viability of a population.[4] It is a way to avoid difficult decisions, but it is management on the brink of disaster and it deprives us of many wildlife values. Some may argue that a fluctuating herd of 2000-3000 bison may not be necessary to maintain the genetic integrity of wild bison. But others have disagreed (Chapter 5). I contend we need some wild bison herds that are large enough to recognize our limited knowledge of bison population genetics and to leave room for error. Therefore, based on current knowledge, plains bison restoration will require some herds that fluctuate between at least 2000 and 3000 animals. In any case, there will be little conservation value in promoting herds of fewer than 1000 wild bison. We already have several small herds (Chapter 11).

How Many Herds and Bison Ranges?

A consortium of wildlife biologists suggested a vision of having about 20 "recovery zones" with wild bison occupying at least 15 major habitat types in the next 50 years.[2] Is this realistic? Only time will tell. I suggest at least one large public reserve with wild bison in each of 5 major ecoregions (Chapter 7). This would be a beginning intended mostly to counter the ongoing domestication of plains bison.

One scenario for the future of wild plains bison would have at least one large herd with a predominance of natural selection to be the core herd in a managed metapopulation in each of the five major ecoregions (Chapter 7). As these herds grow, some bison would periodically be moved into surrounding regional conservation herds to offset effects of genetic drift and domestication in the smaller herds.

Naysayers, particularly in the livestock industry, fear any establishment of wild bison habitat. They view any new bison habitat as a foot in the door that may lead to extensive losses of livestock range. They ask at the beginning, "How much bison range is enough?" This question must be repeatedly answered by each succeeding generation of Americans – owners of the public lands. The current policy of avoiding "any foot in the door" denies those generations their right to answer the question in their own time.

Habitat Quality

It will be tempting to restore wild plains bison with minimal economic expense and maximum avoidance of political controversy. We could relegate more bison to badlands, semi-deserts, sand plains, mountains, and yet another site with radioactive contamination [5] – places left over after the better soils and more productive areas have been claimed for livestock production and agriculture, or places too dangerous for other uses. Relegating bison to suboptimal habitats will leave us with suboptimal bison herds. This palliative concession should be avoided.

Roundups and Culling

Today, most bison in our conservation herds are limited with periodic roundups and selective culling or sale (Chapter 11). This option is less than satisfactory as it fosters domestication and converts live public bison to private ownership, which is a bad precedent for our wildlife. We will continue with roundups and culling on small bison ranges and in areas without effective predators and where public hunting is not suitable, especially for reasons of public safety. However, the emphasis on removing prime-age bison, as practiced in commercial herds and in many conservation herds, is replacing or weakening natural selection for wild characteristics and fosters domestication. To maximize wildness, culling should be randomly directed at young animals, especially yearlings, with most or all older animals allowed to die naturally on the range. The rationale for this strategy is discussed further below, under the topic of public hunting.

Cattle Introgression

Every cattle gene in a bison has replaced a gene that once existed in a wild bison. High levels of cattle gene introgression in bison, sometimes greater than 5% of all genetic markers analyzed, are unacceptable for esthetic as well as biological reasons. Some may promote a standard of 100% purity for wild bison. It is a standard based almost entirely on esthetics. Limited cattle introgression in bison can be invisible, detected only with sophisticated DNA analysis. A pure-bison standard would greatly limit our options for source herds to use in bison restoration. Introgression of cattle genes in the bison genome is so widespread that we cannot simply discard all bison carrying cattle genes without sacrificing some bison alleles that are found only in animals with some introgression.

Yet, it is desirable to purge the bison genome of cattle genes, especially any cattle genes that reduce bison fitness in a wild, natural environment. Current policy is to isolate the few plains bison herds that we believe have no cattle introgression, at least until the genetic technology and genetic knowledge of each bison herd are advanced so that (1) selective purging of cattle genes becomes possible and (2) selected animals may be moved from introgressed herds with confidence that cattle genes are not being transferred. The problem with waiting for genetic knowledge and technology to accumulate is that most conservation herds have cattle introgression and are currently subjected to artificial selection leading to domestication and, I believe, reduction or loss of genes related to wildness.

Probably, most cattle genes will reduce fitness of bison for living in wild environments. If wildness of bison is our goal, these cattle genes are unacceptable. But the problem is also the solution. Natural selection in a wild environment will gradually purge the bison genome of such deleterious cattle genes.[6] We can begin restoring wild bison with animals having no more than, say, 1-2% cattle introgression and let nature take its course in a wild environment. The future of selection and evolution is more important for restoring wild bison than is cattle gene introgression. Introgression should not divert attention from dealing with the more serious and difficult limit to rewilding

214

plains bison.

Predators

American wildlife policy has been evolving to recognize the sometimes harsh realities and complexities of wildness. There was a time when wild animals were either "the good ones" or "the bad ones"; and predators were the bad ones. We killed all species of hawks (so-called "chicken hawks") on sight and we controlled large predators, even in our national parks. Today, we recognize the valuable roles of predators in wild ecosystems and our predator management practices are more flexible. Predator control is a management tool to be applied at times and in places according to varying wildlife conservation goals. But predator control is not appropriate everywhere, and especially not in most of our national parks where the mandate is to leave whole ecosystems intact and unimpaired for future generations of Americans.

Today, plains bison exist with effective predators only in Canada and in the Yellowstone area. Large predators exist in these areas only because they are places where conflicts, especially with livestock, are least likely. Tolerance for wolves and bears outside these zones is minimal and would be even more controversial in grassland environments where cattle predominate everywhere.

Wolves have been a predominant predator in the recent evolution of plains bison. Over several decades, we learned to live with wolves in parts of Minnesota. Now, we are testing the tolerance and management methods for wolves in the Rocky Mountains. It will take decades to determine if natural predators will influence much of the future genome of wild plains bison in the USA. However, nearly-wild bison without wolves will be preferred over having no wild bison.

We will not be able to control the distribution of wild bison without controlling their numbers. For wildness sake, natural predation is the preferred mechanism to limit numbers of bison. Predators, especially wolves, detect many disabilities in their prey and tend to remove the weakest individuals. They are a major factor in maintaining genetic fitness of prey. Wherever wild bison are to be restored without wolves, which will be most areas for the foreseeable future, public hunting should be the next best option, applied with caution as described below.

Disease Management

Our wildlife policy has yet to deal with the issue of wildlife disease. Why is wildlife evolution with predators appropriate in some wild places, whereas wildlife evolution with disease is not? In essence, are diseases not just predators designed small? One may argue that bison diseases are transmittable to livestock. But so are wolves and bears. We have reserved a few places for wolves and bears. Are there to be no places where bison and their diseases may continue to evolve and adapt to each other? If the answer is no, we are neglecting the values of coevolution and are committing bison and ourselves to perpetual, expensive management of wildlife diseases, and to moving bison toward domestication (Chapter 8).

When diseases are transmittable between livestock and wildlife, the livestock industry often proposes wildlife reduction or annihilation, and/or application of domestic animal health treatments to wildlife. The industry dismisses the value of coevolution and the public costs. In promoting these self-serving solutions, the risks of disease transmission to livestock may be exaggerated. The issue of transmittable diseases has sometimes been used as a convenient excuse more than a rational reason to oppose restoration of wild bison. However, the primary place for controlling livestock disease should be in livestock management, not in wildlife management. That said, complicated disease issues should not be neglected in bison restoration. But if we wait for the ultimate technological solutions, we will never have wild bison.

To Restore Wild Plains Bison

Public Hunting for Population Control

We have more wild horses than wild bison on our public lands. However, laws do not permit harvest of wild horses. Limiting the numbers of wild horses on our public lands with roundups, sales and prolonged constricted pasturing and feeding has become a permanent public-money pit. This is not a model we want to follow for bison.

Bison co-evolved with human hunting as a major selective force in their recent evolution (Chapter 1). Today, strategically managed hunting should help to maintain, not diminish, wildness of bison. Public hunting cannot nearly replace natural predation as a selective force removing animals that subtly display weaknesses which often have a genetic connection. Worse, trophy hunting has potential to selectively remove the fittest males before their dominance is expressed when they become old enough to compete for breeding cows. Where wildness is a goal, and especially where natural predators are rare or absent, hunting regulations should direct the harvest away from the fittest animals and toward a more non-selective taking of animals such that hunting becomes a more neutral selective force. For this purpose, regulated public hunting should be directed towards the youngest and oldest bison. This simulates selection of prey by natural predators; but the justification for this strategy is more complicated than that.

In a wildlife population, reproductive potential declines with age. Young animals may yet breed and pass on their genes many times in their lifetime. Old animals have most or all their breeding behind them. Concurrently in the aging process, as bison compete and natural selection operates on one age-cohort over the years, the ratio of more-fit animals to less-fit animals is expected to increase. Usually, this change in the proportion of more-fit to less-fit bison begins very gradually after the first year of life because mortality rates for bison between 1 and perhaps 4 years of age tend to be small. However each year, natural selection removes some of the less fit animals. As a result, the oldest animals have most demonstrated their fitness for survival in the prevailing environment.

The practice of selecting mid-age bulls – about 5 years old, because they provide, in the eyes of some hunters, the best trophy mounts, and the practice of harvesting prime-age cows, will have the most negative impact in replacing or weakening natural selection that otherwise would remove mostly the less fit bison. This is because 1) the proportion of more fit bison in a cohort goes up with age, increasing the probability of taking a more fit animal with a non selective harvest from an older age class; and 2) prime-age bison still have many years of reproduction in which to pass along their genes.

In contrast, harvest of the oldest bison will have little or no impact upon natural selection because these animals have little or no reproductive potential left in their lifetime. However, harvesting only the oldest bison may not control herd numbers because there are relatively few old bison.

At the other extreme, random harvest of the youngest animals, while removing those with the most remaining reproductive potential, will be taking bison at an age when the proportion of less fit individuals in the age cohort is greatest. Thus, there is less chance of taking a more-fit bison that "should" survive and reproduce for the most number of subsequent years. But how would we apply this strategy?

In bison hunting to emphasize wildness of the herd, killing of calves, as wolves often do, will be abhorrent to both hunters and non hunters. However, taking of yearlings should be emphasized. Yearling bison will be 16-20 months old during a fall or winter hunting season. Yearlings are large enough to provide significant amounts of meat, yet not so large as to create serious logistical problems in processing the carcasses. Yearling bison are relatively easy for hunters to distinguish in the field to comply with prescriptive hunting regulations.

Random (non selective) harvest of bison will contribute to genetic drift and loss of rare alleles (Chapter 5). This negative impact of public hunting will have to be diminished by maintaining a large bison herd.

Bison hunting will provide unique challenges to hunting ethics and to the administration of public hunting. Methods used for other big game likely will not suffice. Bison are our largest big game. They travel in large herds, usually in open habitat. Aspects of hunting that are difficult for hunters or are distressing to some citizens are magnified with bison. Once a bison is down, the logistics of processing the carcass and transporting the valuable parts become more than a lone hunter can usually handle. Harvested bison leave very large unsightly gut piles, the persistence of which will depend upon the local abundance of scavengers. Gut piles may attract dangerous predators, such as grizzly bears, to areas where they are unwelcome. Herd behavior of bison, and their open habitat, may foster competition among hunters concurrently in the field, diminishing the hunting experience and encouraging less careful selection of animals and shot placements. Surrounding Yellowstone National Park, a migratory segment of the Park bison herd invades Montana after the normal big game hunting season has ended. Any need to limit this herd segment will bring up ethical questions of hunting when cows are in mid- to late-pregnancy. This latter issue may be handled by directing harvest to some bulls and to many yearlings, as yearlings will not be pregnant.

These and other issues of bison hunting will require creative methods for dispersing hunters in time and space, for limiting the locations where bison are killed, for controlling the sexes and ages of harvested bison, and for allowing removal of bison in ways that do not have negative impacts on the landscape. Best methods will be site-specific and will be developed from experience with the behavior of hunters and bison. Since bison hunting is a logistical challenge, family hunts should be encouraged.

Such strategic harvesting practices will place considerable obligation on hunters. They must carefully identify the sex and age of their prey before pulling the trigger. It will be part of the definition of ethical hunting – understanding the needs of the prey population and observing ethical obligations to future generations of hunters and others who will want to use and enjoy wild bison.

These ideas deserve more discussion among wildlife conservation biologists and managers. In any case, where maintenance of wildness is a population goal, and hunting is the predominant form of mortality, hunting should be applied in a way that does not greatly alter the natural sex- and age-structure of the bison herd. Furthermore, many bison should die naturally on the range.

It is in the interest of the hunting community to participate in discussions of bison restoration, and to compel state executives and agencies to address the issues. Otherwise, unlike all other big game, public bison hunting will remain largely an activity of the past. But there is danger that, once established, public hunting of bison will develop a constituency with a narrow, self-serving focus. Used and valued for its contribution to wildness, hunting should be part of the restoration process, not an end in itself. For major plains bison restoration projects, the goal of harvesting animals should be subordinate to the goal of wildness of bison and of bison habitat.

Legal Status of Bison

Any future for wild plains bison will require legal recognition of bison as wildlife. Most states do not recognize wild bison. In these states, conservation herds have limited futures until state laws are modified. Perhaps more than any other factor, the restoration of wild plains bison awaits a politically active constituency in each state where restoration will occur. However, to gain acceptance, each constituency will have to address the issues cited above, and explain them to opponents and to the larger number of citizens who have never considered these issues surrounding the future of wild bison.

The federal government, representing all the people, currently seems unlikely to restore wild plains bison on federal lands without support from an affected state. This could change if the Fish and Wildlife Service would recognize the threat of domestication to the future of the wild bison genome and list plains bison as a threatened or endangered species. However, the mere threat of federal listing might change attitudes within a state government.

It remains to be seen if the federal government can provide persistent and effective leadership to develop federal-state cooperation in restoring wild plains bison. An urban movement, from both east and west coasts, may be necessary to promote and sustain federal efforts. As when bison were first saved from oblivion, states in the center of the continent seem unable to counter opposition to bison restoration from the livestock industry. If this is true, then a majority of Americans, from eastern states and the west coast, must demand bison restoration as a federal project on federal lands. Hopefully, citizens of the central states will participate.

Adaptive Management

We don't have all the answers for managing wild bison. However, if we wait for all the answers, we will never restore wild bison. Only after beginning the restoration process, can we learn what all the questions, let alone all the answers, are. We must go to learn, and learn as we go.

Footnotes:

[1] Leopold (1933).

[2] Sanderson et al. (2008).

[3] Gates et al. (2010).

[4] Redford et al. (2011).

[5] One of our conservation herds is on the former Rocky Mountain Arsenal, Colorado. This area has contaminated soils. Under current rules, any bison removed from the Arsenal may not be consumed.

[6] Geist (1991) suggested that limited cattle-gene introgression in bison is not a disaster if we will allow natural selection to purge the herds in favor of wild characteristics.

Epilogue

Land, the Bottom Line

In 2010, Joe Gutkosky, friend and retired Forest Service employee, floated through the Upper Missouri River Breaks National Monument. Of course, he saw no bison where Lewis and Clark once saw many thousands. But he estimates he saw about 1000 cattle, "almost everywhere" along the river banks and in the river. This illustrates the status of "multiple use" on our federal lands in the West. We have cattle almost everywhere, even in recreation areas and on wildlife refuges, and wild bison nowhere.

To its credit, the livestock industry is mostly united for its self interest, and is politically effective. Moreover, it has a marketing program that promotes the industry and its needs at all levels of public discourse. Subtle propaganda implies that ranch families are all hard-working religious people with strong family values, and that whatever is good for them is good for all. This industry controls much public thought as well as public land.

Putting together a few large, public ranges for wild bison and other prairie species will not come easily. There are obvious areas of largely public land to consider. The need is urgent, for bison must be losing wildness with each generation, even if we do not recognize the change. First, we must discard the idea that our public lands are to be managed primarily to satisfy the needs of nearby private lands. This is tyranny of a minority. The majority public owners of public lands deserve the same rights as do private owners on private lands.

Some will say that restoring wild plains bison is a stalking horse for reintroducing wolves in some areas. I contend wolves are a separate issue that will be addressed whether or not we restore wild bison. True, a restored bison herd will be more wild, in the sense promoted here, if it lives with wolves. But a restored wild bison herd without wolves is far better than no wild bison. We should restore wild bison with, or if necessary, without wolves. I think future generations of Americans will agree.

Some may ask, "Why restore wild plains bison?" I have tried to

Epilogue

answer this question in terms of public values (Chapter 6). However, when considering opportunities for ourselves and for future generations, we should be asking, "Why not restore wild plains bison?" Answers to the latter question often demonstrate the self-interests of naysayers who seek maximum control over public lands and public wildlife.

Public Awareness

A brochure obtained at the National Bison Range, Montana reads: "The American buffalo which by 1890 was threatened with extinction, has been preserved and its numbers increased until there are now over 250,000 in North America." I have read similar words at other visitor centers around the country. One brochure proclaims that we now have bison in all 50 states. (I am so glad there are bison in Hawaii!) The signs, websites and brochures, both public and private, usually paint a rosy picture of the status of plains bison. Many seek public approval and funding for their efforts in warehousing and domesticating bison. They wrongfully promote the impression that plains bison conservation was accomplished long ago. They do little, often nothing, to promote public understanding of bison domestication and of the meaning, values and requirements of wildness. They foster complacency when alarm bells should be ringing.

Public apathy is the ultimate barrier to restoring wild plains bison on native range in the USA. Wild bison will not be saved by scientists. Their job is to create a public awareness of the needs and methods for conserving wild bison. Only broad public advocacy can save wild bison in the United States.

Professional Indifference

American plains bison are a magnificent gift of evolution that traces back to ice-age time. Out of the past, Charles Darwin screams to us, "Bison will not retain their wild character unless their continued evolution occurs in a wild environment."

Yet, most professional wildlife biologists neglect the meaning and value of wildness and concentrate on interventionist management. This is somewhat understandable. Many are doing what they were taught in schools of wildlife management. Also, they are doing what they are paid for, as most funding for most biologists comes from hunters and anglers. I was one of them for much of my career.

The plea for wildness is not to replace the wildlife management paradigm. It is a plea to expand thought and practice to embrace a broader array of goals for our wildlife. Intensive management has its place. Wildness should also have a place.

Looking Ahead

Some may suggest that my plea for restoring wild bison is "living in the past." Such thinking presumes that values of the future must replace all values of the past. I must reply, why not have both, to the extent that we can? We have not thrown away Mozart and Tchaikovsky to embrace rock-and-roll, Swan Lake for modern dance, Mark Twain for Tony Hillerman! Do we burn all the old books in all the libraries because we have new books? Why monotonize the world? Since we have large tracts of public land, why should we have domestic cattle and domestic landscapes almost everywhere and wild bison nowhere? Why throw away wild plains bison, for all time, because restoration may be troublesome in the current world? With effort, we can restore wild plains bison on some wild grasslands in the USA for those who will use, understand and appreciate their unique values. The long-term costs will not be great, and the values of wild bison will soon be irreplaceable.

It is my hope that this book will help to shatter the widespread perception that bison are "alright", because they were saved by Theodore Roosevelt and there are lots of bison today. Probably, I will never know if I succeed. The future of wildness in plains bison is in other, younger hands.

References

Adams, S. M. and A. R. Dood. 2011. Background Information on Issues of Concern for Montana: Plains Bison Ecology, Management, and Conservation. Montana Fish, Wildlife & Parks, Helena, MT.

Aguirre, A. A. and E. E. Starkey. 1994. Wildlife disease in U. S. National Parks: Historical and coevolutionary perspectives. Conservation Biology 8:654-661.

Belue, T. F. 1996. The Long Hunt: Death of the Buffalo East of the Mississippi. Stackpole Books, Mechanicsburg, PA.

Boyd, D. P. 2003. Conservation of North American bison: Status and Recommendations. PhD Thesis, Univ. Calgary, Alberta.

Bragg, T. K., B. Hamilton and A. Steuter. 2002. Guidelines for bison management, The Nature Conservancy, Arlington, Virginia.

Brinkley, D. 2009. The Wilderness Warrior: Theodore Roosevelt and the Crusade for America. HarperCollins Publishers, New York.

Burroughs, R. D. 1961. The Natural History of the Lewis and Clark Expedition. Michigan St. Univ. Press, East Lansing, MI.

Butler, B. R. 1978. Bison hunting in the desert West before 1800: the paleo-ecological potential and the archaeological reality. The Plains Anthropologist 23:106-112.

Cahalane, V. H. 1947. Mammals of North America. Macmillan Co. New York, NY.

Callenbach, E. 1996. Bring Back the Buffalo: A Sustainable Future for America's Great Plains. Univ. California Press, Berkeley.

Carriker, R. C. 1995. Father Peter John DeSmet, Jesuit in the West. Univ. Oklahoma Press, Norman, OK.

Christopherson, R. J., R. J. Hudson and R. J. Richmond. 1978. Comparative winter bioenergetics of American bison, yak, Scottish Highland and Hereford calves. Acta Theriologica 23:49-54.

References

Christopherson, R. J., R. J. Hudson and M. K. Christopherson. 1979. Seasonal energy expenditures and thermoregulatory response of bison and cattle. Canadian J. Animal Science 59:611-617.

Clutton-Brock, J. 1999. A natural history of domesticated mammals. Cambridge Univ. Press, Cambridge, UK.

Coppedge, B. R. 2009. Patterns of bison hair use in nests of tallgrass prairie birds. The Prairie Naturalist 41:110-115.

Coppedge, B. R. 2010. Bison hair reduces predation on artificial bird nests. Oklahoma Ornithological Society Bulletin 43:13-16.

Covey, C. 1993. Cabeza DeVaca's Adventures in the Unknown Interior of America. Univ. New Mexico Press, Albuquerque, NM.

Cronin, M. A., M. D. MacNeil, N. Vu, V. Leesburg, H. D. Blackburn and J. N. Derr. 2013. Genetic variation and differentiation of bison (*Bison bison*) subspecies and cattle (*Bos taurus*) breeds and subspecies. J. Heredity 104:500-509.

Dary, D. A. 1974. The Buffalo Book. Ohio Univ. Press, Miami, OH.

Daubenmire, R. 1985. The western limits of the range of the American bison. Ecology 66:622-624.

Derr, J. N., P. W. Hedrick, N. D. Halbert, L. Plough, L. K. Dobson, J. King, C. Duncan, D. L. Hunter, N. D. Cohen and D. Hedgecock. 2012. Phenotypic effects of cattle mitochondrial DNA in American bison. Conservation Biology 26:1130-1136.

Donnelly, J. P. 1967. Wilderness Kingdom, Indian Life in the Rocky Mountains: 1840-1847. The Journals & Paintings of Nicolas Point. Holt, Rinehart and Winston, NY.

Dratch, P. A. and P. J. Gogan. 2010. Bison Conservation Initiative: Bison conservation workshop, report and recommendations. U. S. Dept. Interior, National Park Service Natural Resource Program Center, Fort Collins, CO.

Evans, H. E. 1997. The Natural History of the Long Expedition to the Rocky Mountains, 1819-1820. Oxford Univ. Press, New York, NY.

References

Franke, M. A. 2005. To Save the Wild Bison: Life on the Edge in Yellowstone. Univ. Oklahoma Press, Norman, OK.

Freese, C. H. et al. 2007. Second chance for the plains bison. Biological Conservation 136:175-184.

Fryxell, M. M. 1928. The former range of the bison in the Rocky Mountains. Journal of Mammalogy 9:129-139.

Fuhlendorf, S. D., B. W. Allred and R. G. Hamilton. 2010. Bison as keystone herbivores on the Great Plains: Can cattle serve as proxy for evolutionary grazing patterns? American Bison Society Working Paper 4:40pp.

Gard, W. 1959. The Great Buffalo Hunt. Univ. Nebraska Press, Lincoln, NE.

Gates, C. C., C. H. Freese, P. J. P. Gogan and M. Kotzman (Eds.) 2010. American Bison: Status Survey and Conservation Guidelines. International Union for Conservation of Nature and Natural Resources. Gland, Switzerland.

Geist, V. 1991. Phantom subspecies: The wood bison *Bison bison "athabascae"* Rhoads 1897 is not a valid taxon, but an ecotype. Arctic 44: 283-300.

Geist, V. 1992. Endangered species and the law. Nature 357:274-276.

Geist, V. 1996. Buffalo Nation: History and Legend of the North American Bison. Voyageur Press, Stillwater, MN.

Gowans, F. R. 1985. Rocky Mountain Rendezvous, A History of the Fur Trade Rendezvous, 1825-1840. Peregrine Smith Books, Layton, UT.

Grayson, D. K. 2006. Holocene bison in the Great Basin, western USA. The Holocene 16:913-925.

References

Gross, J. E., G. Wang, N. D. Halbert, P. A. Gogan, J. N. Derr and J. W. Templeton. 2006. Effects of population control strategies on retention of genetic diversity in National Park Service bison (*Bison bison*) herds. Revised final report, Dept. of Biology, Montana St. Univ., Bozeman.

Guthrie, R. D. 1990. Frozen Fauna of the Mammoth Steppe. Univ. Chicago Press, Chicago, IL.

Hafen, L. R. 1965, Mountain Men and Fur Traders of the Far West. Univ. Nebraska Press, Lincoln, NE.

Haines, A. L. (Ed.). 1965. Osborne Russell's Journal of a Trapper. Univ. Nebraska Press, Lincoln, NE.

Halbert, N. D., P. J. Gogan, P. W. Hedrick, J. M. Wahl and J. N. Derr. 2012. Genetic population substructure in bison at Yellowstone National Park. J. Heredity 103:1-11.

Hasselstrom, L. M. 1984. James Clyman, Journal of a Mountain Man. Mountain Press, Missoula, MT.

Hawley, A. W. L., D. G. Peden and W. R. Stricklin. 1981. Bison and Hereford steer digestion on sedge hay. Canadian J. Animal Sci. 61:165-174.

Hedrick, P. W. 2009. Conservation genetics and North American Bison (*Bison bison*). J. of Heredity. Advance access printing.

Isenberg, A. C. 2000. The Destruction of the Bison. Cambridge Univ. Press, Cambridge, UK.

Jones, J. D., J. J. Treanor and R. L. Wallen. 2009. Parturition in Yellowstone bison. Final Report, Yellowstone Center for Resources, Yellowstone National Park, Wyoming.

Jones, L. C. and T. J. Roffe. 2008. Management of bison in the National Wildlife Refuge System, US Fish and Wildlife Service. Unpublished USFWS report.

References

Knapp, A. K., J. M. Blair, J. M. Briggs, S. L. Collins, D. C. Hartnett, L. C. Johnson and E. G. Towne. 1999. The keystone role of bison in North American tallgrass prairie. BioScience 49:39-50.

Kurten, B. and E. Anderson. 1980. Pleistocene Mammals of North America. Columbia Univ. Press, NY.

Lavender, D. 1963. Westward Vision, The Story of the Oregon Trail. Univ. Nebraska Press, Lincoln, NE.

Leopold, A. 1933. Game Management. Charles Scribner's Sons, New York.

Leopold, A. 1953. Round River: from the Journals of Aldo Leopold. Oxford University Press.

Lott, D. F. 2002. American Bison. Univ. California Press, Berkeley, CA.

Lyman, R. L. 2004. Late-quaternary diminution and abundance of prehistoric bison (*Bison* sp.) in eastern Washington state, USA. Quaternary Research 62:76-85.

Manning, R. 2009. Rewilding the West: Restoration in a Prairie Landscape. Univ. California Press, Berkeley, CA.

Meagher, M. M. 1973. The Bison of Yellowstone National Park. National Park Service Scientific Monograph No. 1. National Park Service, Washington, DC.

Merriam, C. H. 1926. The buffalo of northeastern California. Journal of Mammalogy 7:211-214.

Meyer, M. E. 1992. *Brucella abortus* in the Yellowstone National Park bison herd. Report to Yellowstone National Park, unpublished.

Nishi, J. S. 2010. A review of best practices and principles for bison disease issues: Greater Yellowstone and Wood Buffalo Areas. Working Paper 3. American Bison Society.

O'Brien, D. 2002. Buffalo for the Broken Heart: Restoring Life to a Black Hills Ranch. Random House, New York, NY.

References

O'Regan, H. J. and A. C. Kitchener. 2005. The effects of captivity on the morphology of captive, domesticated and feral mammals. Mammal Reviews 35:215-230.

Perez-Figueroa, A., T. Antao, J. A. Coombs and G. Luikart. 2010. Conserving genetic diversity in Yellowstone bison: effects of population fluctuations and variance in male reproductive success in age structured populations. Technical Rpt. Yellowstone National Park, National Park Service, Wyoming.

Phillips, P. C. (Ed.). 1940. Life in the Rocky Mountains by W. A. Ferris. The Old West Publ. Co., Denver, CO. (original not seen).

Popper, D. E. and F. J. Popper. 1987. The great plains: from dust to dust. Planning 53:2-18.

Redford, K. H. et al. 2011. What does it mean to successfully conserve a (vertebrate) species? Bioscience 61:39-48.

Roden, C., H. Vervaecke and L. Van Elsacker. 2005. Dominance, age and weight in American bison males (*Bison bison*) during non-rut in semi-natural conditions. Applied Animal Behaviour Science 92:169-177.

Sanderson, E. W. et al. 2008. The ecological future of the North American bison: conceiving long-term, large-scale conservation of wildlife. Conservation Biology 22:252-266.

Seabury, C. M., N. D. Halbert, P. J. P. Gogan, J. W. Templeton and J. N. Derr. 2005. Bison *PRNP* genotyping and potential association with *Brucella* spp. seroprevalence. Animal Genetics 36:104-110.

Shaw, J. H. and M. Lee. 1997. Relative abundance of bison, elk, and pronghorn on the southern plains, 1806-1857. Plains Anthropologist 42:163-172.

Shaw, J. H. and M. Meagher. 2000. Bison. Pp. 447-466 in S. Demarais and P. R. Krausman (Eds.). Ecology and Management of Large Mammals in North America. Prentice-Hall, Inc. NJ.

Smith, V. G. 1997. The Champion Buffalo Hunter, The Frontier Memoirs of Yellowstone Vic Smith (J. Prodgers, Ed.). Globe Pequot

References

Press, Guilford, CN.

Traill, L. W., B. W. Brook, R. R. Frankham and C. J. A. Bradshaw. 2009. Pragmatic population viability targets in a rapidly changing world. Biological Conservation 143:28-34.

Van Vuren, D. 1987. Bison west of the Rocky Mountains: an alternative explanation. Northwest Science 61:65-69.

Van Vuren, D. and M. P. Bray. 1985. The recent geographic distribution of *Bison bison* in Oregon. The Murrelet 66:56-58.

Van Vuren, D. and F. C. Dietz. 1993. Evidence of *Bison bison* in the Great Basin. Great Basin Naturalist 53:318-319.

Vestal, S. 1952. Joe Meek, The Merry Mountain Man. Univ. Nebraska Press, Lincoln, NE.

Woolhouse, M. E. J, J. P. Webster, E. Domingo, B. Charlesworth and B. R. Levin. 2002. Biological and biomedical implications of the co-evolution of pathogens and their hosts. Nature Genetics 32:569-577.

Zontek, K. 2007. Buffalo Nation: American Indian Efforts to Restore the Bison. Univ. Nebraska Press, Lincoln, NE.

Index

Index

Index